STOP BEING A BROKE LOSER

By Christopher Alan Bell

Table of Contents

A Brief Introduction

Chapter 1: Change Your Mindset — 9

Chapter 2: Cash Management (Budgeting/Revenue/Expenses) — 21

Chapter 3: Risk Mitigation (AKA Insurance) — 37

Chapter 4: Investing (Stocks/Bonds/Alternatives) — 56

Chapter 5: Do not Invest Like a Dude-Bro (Bitcoin/Gold/Options/Penny Stocks) — 87

Chapter 6: Don't Pay Taxes on Your Investments (IRA, 401K, 529s) — 101

Chapter 7: Only Get Married to Have Children. If You Do Get Married, Get a Prenup — 116

Chapter 8: Children Do not Have to Cost $250,000 — 122

Chapter 9: Use Credit Cards to Build Your Credit Score and Build Wealth — 133

Chapter 10: Ditch the Home with the White Picket Fence — 145

Chapter 11: Cars Are Your Enemy — 165

Chapter 12: Fire Your Scummy Financial Advisor — 174

Chapter 13: Student Loans are Toxic Trash — 192

Chapter 14: Join the Military — 202

Chapter 15: Exercise and Eat Healthy — 221

Chapter 16: Have a Plan for Retirement — 228

Conclusion — 233

A Brief Introduction

If you needed a $1,200 stimulus check to pay your bills on time during the Coronavirus pandemic, you are a **BROKE LOSER**. A sad, despicable mess. Judgmental? Yes. A nice thing to say? No. The Unabashed Truth? Yep.

No, I am not talking about a family of four living below the Federal poverty line, which is a meager $26,200 in 2020[1]. I understand it is almost impossible to save money on such a low income, and I feel sympathy for workers and their families who live on such a paltry income. I also have sympathy for people whose life circumstances <u>out of their control</u> have put them in dire financial straits. For example, getting cancer and cashing out your life savings to pay for treatment is out of your control.

Going into massive student loan debt for a worthless degree, quitting college or trade school because "it was too hard, boo hoo" or just being lazy is totally in your control, and puts you solidly in the **BROKE LOSER** category. The median American household pulls in a healthy $61,937 per year. If you belong to such a family, and you did not have the savings to pay your bills after only a month or two on

---

1- [1] https://aspe.hhs.gov/poverty-guidelines - **Poverty line**

unemployment, you are a financial failure and deserve to be mocked relentlessly.

Any American that is not living in abject poverty has no excuse to not have a fully funded emergency savings account. In America, personal finance gurus are a dime-a-dozen, and all of them recommend you set aside three to six months of expenses in case you lose your job, or you have an unexpected, large expense. Smart Americans listen to their advice and make small sacrifices to reduce their spending and save money. These Americans are intelligent enough to understand the concept of deferring gratification, of sacrificing pleasure in the short-term to achieve long-term benefits. These are the rare breed of American who are functional adults, who have the self-control to take charge of their finances like big boys and girls.

These financially responsible Americans are a rare breed. The far less intelligent, and much more common American, is the American that spends every dime they make. They live only for short-term pleasure and are wholly incapable of understanding they will be alive at a future date. To this American, budgeting is a boring and useless concept that only cheap asses do, but blowing all your money on a car, boat, RV, or gun collection is a sign of success. It never occurs to this American that saving your money allows you to go on more adventures and be able to afford more things than a person who never saves their money could ever do.

Let me be clear; your income has **nothing** to do with whether you are a failure and loser. What you do **with** that income is what separates the rich from the poor, the successful from the failures. I DO NOT respect a person based on how much they make. I DO respect people for their propensity to save, or their ability to defer gratification and save a certain percentage of their income, regardless of how much they make.

You make $150,000 a year, but have no savings? **BROKER LOSER.** You make $40,000 a year, but have $50,000 in savings and $150,000 in stock mutual funds? **WINNER.** Pretty easy to understand. It is easier for a person making $500,000 to save $10,000 in a rainy-day fund than it is for someone making $40,000, but in both examples, it is achievable. It is just a matter of time and will-power.

Americans are the epitome of horrible personal finances. In Dec 2019, before Corona started its rampage in the USA, the average American personal savings rate was 7.5%. This spiked up to 13.1% in March 2020, but only after the virus resulted in mass lay-offs and job market uncertainty[2]. Saving 7.5% of your income, on average, is pitifully low. With such a low savings rate, the average 18-34-year-old in American only has a median of $1,000 in a savings account, and the median 35-44-year-old only has $2,500.[3] Sad, sad, SAD. I can give some leniency to the younger age bracket for not having much saved up, but for someone between age 35-44, you should be a big boy or girl by now and understand that you need money set aside to protect yourself and loved ones from financial catastrophe.

When I was in my 20s, I was made fun of for saving money. I was called "cheap," "Shylock," "Scrooge," "stupid" and many other things because I dared to save and invest a portion of my paycheck instead of blowing it on meaningless junk. Yes, I lived around some real winners back in the day. If you adjust your financial habits after reading this book, you will, like me, most likely encounter the same vitriol from your friends and family. If you choose to save a higher percentage of your income, you will have to cut back on your standard of living.

This will invite disparaging comments from everyone, who will try to guilt you for getting your life on track. You

---

[2] https://www.statista.com/statistics/246268/personal-savings-rate-in-the-united-states-by-month/
[3] https://www.nerdwallet.com/blog/banking/savings-account-balances-by-age-how-do-you-compare/

will be called a "Cheap-ass" "scrooge" or "Mr. Penny Pincher." It will happen, trust me. And that is fine. American consumer culture is antithetical to good personal finances because the financial system's health and corporate profitability hinge on consumers spending everything they make. Most Americans cannot fathom a lifestyle that does not involve blowing every dollar they get their hands on, because they have been taught to do so from birth. Believe in yourself, because fixing your financial situation will improve your chances of attaining happiness in life; ignore haters and losers who will try to shame you.

I want this book to inspire Americans to change their financial futures for the better. To help them understand their salary is irrelevant to achieving financial security. That there are high earners who are flat broke, and low wage earners who are secretly wealthy. That poverty and wealth are a mindset, not something that is inherited or given through privilege. That anybody can change their current financial situation for the better, regardless of how bad they think they have it.

If you think you have the **BROKE LOSER** mindset and you want to replace it with something better, this is the book for you. If you want to stay a **BROKER LOSER**, you can toss this in the trash. You will learn basic personal finance principles, such as balancing the competing priorities of cash, investments, and insurance management. You will learn how to avoid common financial traps, like buying a house or a car you cannot afford. Enjoy!

Chapter 1: Change Your Mindset

Changing your mindset is the first step to getting out of the financial mess you are in. The difference between a successful person and a **BROKE LOSER** is how they view money, not how much they make. Your salary is irrelevant. The size of your house or car is irrelevant. Your stupid boat and RV is irrelevant. Your balance sheet and personal net worth are the only things that differentiate between a success and a failure in the realm of personal finance. The **BROKER LOSER** asks others "How much do you make?" The **RICH WINNER** asks, "What's your net worth?"

Leave your communist, capital-hating propaganda at the door. Money is not the root of all evil; money is the tool that will make you happy, secure, and at peace with the world. Being frugal does not mean you are cheap. Money is FREEDOM. Money CAN buy happiness.

You must see money as something to save and use to build you empire, not something to consume. Your biweekly paycheck is NOT to be spent as fast as possible on short-term pleasures and frivolous nonsense. Your paycheck IS an opportunity to buy things that generate a bigger paycheck for you and your family in the future. What can you buy that generates more money for your family over the long term? You can buy <u>bonds</u>, which pay your interest payments. You can buy <u>stocks</u>, which generate cash flow through dividends. You can buy <u>real estate</u> and rent it out, hopefully generating positive cash flow through rental income. You can pay a professional resume writer to spruce up your competitiveness for that job interview you need to nail to increase your income. Every day, you choose to either spend your money to buy things that make you more money, or to buy things for short-term pleasure.

Imagine you have a choice to purchase one of two machines. Machine 1 costs $100, and when you bring it home and plug it in, it starts spitting out a fresh $1 bill every month. Machine 1 also appreciates in value, so if you choose to sell it a year down the road, you can sell it for $112. Machine 2 also costs $100, but instead of spitting out a $1 bill every month, it requires you to put a $1 bill into it every month to keep it running. Machine 2 goes down in value every year, and after a year it is only worth $80 in resale value.

What machine would you rather buy? Everyone would, of course, buy Machine 1. It pays you every month AND it goes up in value. Machine 2 does the exact opposite. Machine 1 is, in personal finance speak, an **asset** because it generates <u>positive</u> cash flow. Machine 2 is a **liability** because it generates <u>negative</u> cash flow. Machine 1 pays you, Machine 2 costs you. You want to spend your money on something that pays you, but that is not what the average American does. They do the exact opposite, spending all on their income to buy as many Machine 2s as they can afford. Why? Because the TV told them to.

If you never use part of your paycheck to buy Machine 1s, you will never build wealth. You will always be a **BROKE LOSER**, living paycheck to paycheck, never progressing in your financial life, dumping everything you make into your growing work-shop full of Machine 2s. You will get your biweekly paycheck, only to watch it vanish into your massive and ever-growing collection of Machine 2s. All of which, on top of consuming your entire paycheck, are dropping in value every single year. The ever-increasing financial demands of your Machine 2s will push you to get a promotion at work or work extra hours, but instead of learning your lesson, you will just keep buying MORE Machine 2s so you can dump MORE cash into them.

After all, TV commercials and social conventions constantly remind you only that if you do not spend everything you make on Machine 2s, you are a LOSER. And so, you keep doing what you are doing, spending your entire life grinding away at work. When you die, your legacy will be a workshop full of worthless Machine 2s. Pretty ridiculous, huh? Well, that's exactly what Americans do.

Do not be that average, boring, unimpressive, **BROKE LOSER** American. Instead of spending your entire paycheck on Machine 2s because the billboard told you to, buy as many Machine 1s as you can. The more you buy, the more money they pay you every month, and the easier it gets to buy even MORE Machine 1s. Your neighbors may scoff at your lack of Machine 2s, but that is okay; most of them cannot sleep at night because they are stressing about keeping their Machine 2s working. Before you know it, you will have so much cash flooding in every month from your Army of Machine 1s that you pay all your bills and support your lifestyle without you having to work.

Once you are there, you can choose to retire if you want to. Or keep working if you like your job; whatever floats your boat. This is all common sense, right? But if it is so common sense, why doesn't everyone in America buy Machine 1s and all get rich? Because corporate propaganda and consumer culture push you into only buying Machine 2s. <u>Your spending is corporate America's Machine 1.</u>

What are Machines 1s, or **assets**, as I like to call them? I already mentioned a few; stocks, bonds, and rental properties. Stock investors buy stocks because they expect corporate earnings to grow over time, increasing the value of the stock. Bonds pay interest payments every six months or annually. Tenants in rental properties pay rent, which you use to pay your mortgage and other expenses and pocket the difference. If you buy something and it pays <u>you</u> more than it costs you, you have an asset.

Now, if you are an accountant reading this, chill out. I am not using the accounting definition of an asset, which is something that provides future economic value that can be measured and expressed in dollars. A Rolls Royce, from an accounting point of view, is an asset because it is something that provides future economic value.

From a personal finance perspective, a Rolls Royce is a liability. Once you drive your new Rollie off the lot, does it start shooting dollar bills out of the glove compartment? NOPE. Quite the opposite; a Rollie will consume an ungodly amount of cash over its useful life. Every month, you pay your car payment, part of which is interest. You also pay your car insurance premium, fill up your gas tank, pay for oil changes, replace the tires, pay personal property taxes, and more.

On top of dumping thousands of dollars into your Rollie every year, it drops precipitously in value on the retail market. After five years, your Rollie might only be worth

$30,000, after you have spent more than $60,000 or $70,000 to purchase and maintain it. All to look cool and impress your equally broke and financially illiterate neighbors. A car falls in the Machine 2, or liability category. You buy it, you put money into it every month and it drops in value. Smart investment, bro.

You want to maximize the amount of money you are directing toward assets and minimize the amount of money you are spending on liabilities. Yes, you need to spend money on a car. It is a necessary evil. Most people do not live within walking distance of their work, and that is fine. I am not asking you to go Hippie-dippy and ride a bike 15 miles each way to and from work. But I am suggesting you buy the cheapest car you can get that is dependable.

Buy a car that gets you from Point A to Point B reliably and safely. You do not need to get a stupid Rolls Royce for your 15-minute commute, or to impress girls that are too young for you. That $500-$600 car payment you would have had spent on your flashy cool-guy car can instead go to fully fund your Roth IRA a year, in which you can buy assets. Minimize essential liabilities, eliminate non-essential liabilities, and use the savings to purchase as many assets as you can. That is your creed. Memorize it, internalize, live it.

Once you understand the personal finance definitions of assets and liabilities, your next step is to dump the idea that you are going to get rich quickly. Building wealth takes time, patience, and diligence. Get-rich-quick schemes are for lazy, **BROKER LOSERS**. A Get-Rich-Quicker (GRQ) thinks they are going to find and invest in the next big thing before anybody else does. They believe success in life comes from gambling your money in dubious investments. That building real wealth requires no sacrifice and hard work. It is a complete load of BS.

What inevitably happens is GRQs lose all their money on a terrible idea or product that nobody wants. These schemes almost always involve a con artist of some kind who makes off with everyone else's money. Ever heard of Bernie Madoff? He was showing his clients amazing investment returns well above the market average, all while he was fleecing them out of billions of dollars.

You should never trust someone promising you low-risk, high reward investments. The less risk you want to take on, the lower your potential returns will be, and vice versa. The S&P 500 stock market index has returned, on average, 10% annually since 1926.[4] If you see a shady, Microsoft

---

[4] https://www.investopedia.com/ask/answers/042415/what-average-annual-return-sp-500.asp

Paint-designed advertisement while you are browsing 4chan offering you 15% or 20% monthly risk-free returns on an investment you've never heard of, you're looking at a complete scam. You are looking at an advertisement designed to fleece dopes and lazy people who think they can build true wealth with no effort. Do not be one of these people. You are not going to become wealthy quickly. You need to internalize this, or you will expect to fix your finances quickly, find out it is not working, and quit. There is no magic button or investment to get you to financial security at the drop of a dime.

If you are in massive debt, you are going to scrimp and save for years and work an extra job or two to pay it off. If you spend all your money on nonsense and liabilities, you are going to experience the pain of reducing your standard of living to free up cash flow for asset purchases. If you have no retirement savings, you are going to contribute to your 401K and IRAs for years before you start seeing large balances. Wealth is not attained with the flick of a switch. If you think otherwise, you are a very unintelligent or lazy person…or both.

But do not worry! I know this all sounds miserable, right? Well, no one is going to force you to act and improve your financial life. The rewards of sacrificing your lifestyle or working extra hours for a few years to attain complete financial security are incalculable, but they do require a little bit of pain and hard work. You can endure that pain for a few years, or you can conclude I am a clueless idiot and toss my book in the trash. That is on you. At the end of the day, nobody cares about you except for your parents, maybe. Changing your life starts with you, and nobody can motivate you to do so except YOU. I can just give you the tools, but you will have to choose to pick them up and use them.

Let us clear something else up. If you believe money is the root of all evil, that all wealthy people are scrooges, that business owners get ahead by screwing people over, you've bought into far-leftist propaganda that will sabotage your chances at achieving any success. Accumulating wealth through hard work, prudence and diligent investing are not evil. Saving a portion of your paycheck every month to buy assets will make you wealthy if you stick to it. Having a fully funded emergency savings account, investing in tax-advantaged accounts for retirement, and saving for your children's college education in a College 529 will result in you building wealth, but it does not make you evil. Anybody that whines about wealth or income inequality but does nothing to fix their condition is the epitome of **BROKE LOSER.**

BROKE LOSERS will try to shame you for saving money by cutting back your lifestyle. If you are not spending your entire paycheck on frivolities, you obviously must be a complete Scrooge. What these clowns cannot seem to grasp is there is a difference between being a cheap Scrooge and being frugal. Frugality is being wise with your money by purchasing items that give value. Being cheap is depriving yourself or your family of a necessity simply because you do not want to buy it, even if you have the means to do so responsibly. Buying a slightly used but safe car to commute to work? FRUGAL. Driving your infant child around in a $500 car with two engine leaks and three flat tires because you do not want to spend a small portion of your substantial savings on a new car? CHEAP.

If nothing I have said has motivated you to take action to improve yourself, consider this. Imagine it is 2030, ten years from now. You have $30,000 in a savings account that you can use to cover any unexpected expenses without using your credit card or raiding your 401K. You have $50,000 invested in low cost, index mutual funds in your Roth IRA that grow tax-free to fund your retirement. You are contributing $10,000 a year to your 401K thanks to your company match, which is now sitting at a balance of $150,000. You have a low-cost life insurance policy that would pay $1,500,000 to your family if you died prematurely. You have no debt except for your mortgage. Your children's college education is almost fully funded because you contribute $100/month to their tax-advantaged College 529 plans.

Now imagine the peace of mind this would give you. Imagine the weight of financial stress coming off your shoulders. Sound like a pipe dream? It is not. You must make some sacrifices in the short term to achieve long term success. Personal finance is so easy to understand, yet so horribly neglected by the average American. That the average American could not get by without a Coronavirus stimulus check is despicable. With some exceptions, most people had the ability to save up enough money over the last few years of a booming economy to support themselves over several months of unemployment. The fact they did not is inexcusable.

Personal finance thought leaders like Dave Ramsey and Suze Orman have been on the airwaves for decades, pounding Americans over the head, telling them to have an emergency fund. Giving them easy, step by step instructions to get their financial lives in order. But most people do not care to listen because they "don't have time," or they are "living their lives" or because "only cheap-asses budget." Then, when the economy collapses, the US taxpayer gets screwed by ever-increasing US government debt and money printing to finance Coronavirus stimulus checks. Savers and bond investors get screwed via inflation and rate cuts by the Fed to add liquidity to the economy.

All of screwing, all this debt, all this nonsense because the average American just does not care about personal finances. It is just too hard to sit down for a few hours to go over your budget. It is just too hard to watch a 10-minute YouTube video to understand how index funds work. It is too much effort to click a few buttons to open a Roth IRA account, even though you spend several hours a day watching stupid cat videos. Well, I have had it with financial ignorance! I am going to break down the three foundational pillars of personal finance, barney style, so even the average lazy American can get on board and take some responsibility for their own personal lives. Write this down: The three pillars of personal finance are <u>Cash Management, Investing,</u> and <u>Risk Mitigation</u>.

Chapter 2: Cash Management

Before we talk about buying insurance and investing for retirement, we need to talk about how you will generate sufficient cash flow to buy them. Your options are to increase your income, reduce your expenses, or both. If you do not pledge to do any of these, you are not going anywhere. You will be broke your whole life and be pitifully poor and dependent on the government in retirement, if you retire at all. You can choose, right now, to work "X" hours a week and be broke forever or work ten extra hours a week and start building your wealth. No excuses.

You are not entitled to a 40-hour work week if your hourly wage is not enough to buy insurance for your family and fund your retirement accounts. Same thing with your expenses. If you are spending everything you make on BS liabilities, your reward will be living in a poverty and misery for the last 20-30 years of your life. You can work long hours in your 70s and 80s because you have no choice, or you can cut some unnecessary expenses in your youth, save money and enjoy the final years of your life.

You can be a drain on your children, crushing their ability to generate wealth because they have to babysit you, or you can free your children to pursue their own destiny and build their own fortunes. Maybe even leave them a legacy. The choice is yours.

So how do you increase your income? In the short term, work more hours at your current job and/or find a new part-time job. In the long-term, you need to become more highly specialized and gain a skill set that increases your hourly wage. The best place to start in the short-term is to work more hours at your current job or get a part-time job. Yes, work sucks, and most sane people want to work 40 hours a week or less so they can free up time to pursue their own passions. But that is not how the world works. The world compensates you based on how valuable and rare your skillset is.

If you take the time to master a highly specialized skill like heart surgery, which most people are incapable of or unwilling to do, you are going to get paid a great hourly wage. If your job is to sweep floors, which anyone can learn to do, you are going to get paid low wages. If your current hours worked equate to a low income that you cannot save money on, you need to work more hours, period. Make $400 a week as a barista? Ask for more hours at your job to up that to $500 a week. That is $400 more dollars a month to work toward financial security/freedom.

If your current job will not let you work more hours, find a part-time job. No job is beneath you. Pizza delivery? Do it. Night shift security guard? Do it. You are not special; do what must be done. Of course, do not be a prostitute or sling drugs; keep it legal, please. Do whatever it takes to make more money. If you are not building wealth right now, you are failing, and need to take immediate action. Leisure, free-time and fun need to take a back-seat until you get your financial house in order. Sure, jumping from 40-hour to 60-hour work week is going to suck horribly and you are going to be exhausted. You are not going to see your friends as much. Your stress levels will increase. But that is a good thing. If you do not start making more money, you are never going to get ahead.

You can struggle for a year or two to get yourself out of a financial hole, or you can stay in that hole your entire life and be poor until the day you die. I guarantee you, it is much, much easier to work hard for a few years to set yourself up for a better life than it is to stay at a mediocre income but easier hours your entire life. You do not want to be the 75-year-old who must work at the local grocery store with arthritis because they did not save money when they were younger.

If you start making any excuses for why you cannot work more hours, then you truly are a **BROKE LOSER**. No one cares about how "the system" is keeping you down unless they are trying to get your vote. You can whine and complain about income inequality and how evil capitalist America is, but that is not going to put more money in your pocket. No one cares about you, and no one is going to help you. Sure, you can listen to politicians who are going to promise you change. But how long is that change going to take? Are you going to wait 20 years for change to happen, or are you going to act now to improve your life? Will that change even happen at all?

You should never count on the government to give you prosperity; your own work ethic and drive will give you more success and financial security than any government ever will. At best, the government can give you the essentials to survive, but it will never give you prosperity will. Only you can do that.

In the short-term, if you are a low-wage worker, working extra hours is your best bet. In the long-term, you want to move yourself up from low-wage/low-skill work to high-wage/high-skill work. Let us say you make $10/hour and work 40 hours a week as a barista. You may work hard, but your job is low-skill and thus commands a low hourly wage. Even if you work more hours, you are still only getting $10 more dollars for each hour worked. If this is you, changes need to be made. Your best bet to rapidly increase your income is to gain a skill that society values and pays high wages for. Note that I said a skillset that SOCIETY values, not what you value. That does not mean you are going to gain a skillset YOU are passionate about, but what pays the big bucks. Just understand you always be in a low paying job for the rest of your life unless you gain a practical skill that pays more on an hourly basis.

How do you get a skillset that pays a higher wage? Your choices are learning a trade or going to college. Trades that pay well include licensed practical nurses, HVAC technicians, home inspectors, plumbers, electricians, dental hygienist, and others[5]. Trades gives you practical skills that are in high demand and pay a livable wage. While trades are not "prestigious," they get the job done and can give you a comfortable life if you put in the hard work. If you do not want to go to a traditional four-year college, trades are the way to go. Now, your family and Marxist friends with college degrees in English may look down on you because you chose not to go into massive debt for a worthless piece of paper, but you can tell them to screw off. The only thing that

---

[5] https://www.indeed.com/career-advice/finding-a-job/highest-paying-trade-jobs

matters is the check you get every month and your satisfaction with your job.

If you like working as a plumber, you make a good wage and you are building your wealth, you are by far superior to 100% of college graduates with useless degrees. Working a trade is like driving a used car. It is not sexy, it does not turn heads, but it gets the job done and is conducive to wealth accumulation. Contrast that to a worthless 4-year college degree like English or Sociology, which you can compare to a sports car. It is shiny, it is nice, it gets complements and turns heads, but it puts you in debt and sucks away any chance you have of accumulating wealth.

As you may have noticed, symbols of status in the United States usually result in you being broke. Someone who graduates with an English and $100,000 in student loan debt will get likes on Facebook, a college graduation party, gifts from grandma and grandpa and will be celebrated. Someone who becomes a plumber will be quietly gossiped about. But who is better off?

Trade school is ONE-FOURTH the average cost of college. You will pay about $33,000 for an entire trade school education and you will have a great chance at finding employment when you graduate. You can pay for your training with a combination of vocational scholarships,

Federal Pell grants and personal savings. You need to take as much time as it takes to find ways to save money for school, even if it involves working over the weekends and delaying school for a year or two.

You do not want to go into debt to attend trade school because student loans cannot be forgiven in bankruptcy. You will thank me for discouraging student loans if you have trouble finding a job after graduation. You will also thank me when you graduate and get a good paying trade job instead of being a **BROKE LOSER** in hundreds of thousands of dollars in debt for a "prestigious" liberal arts degree. Your income from your trade job will allow you to start building wealth and achieving financial success. When you are 62 and comfortably retired, you can laugh at your Walmart-greeter peers who must work for the rest of their lives because they derailed their financial futures to get a their prestigious master's in communications degree that got them a minimum wage job at Starbucks at 26 years old.

Going to a four-year college for a degree that lands you a well-paying job after graduation is another option if you want a practical skill but do not want to do blue-collar trade work. That is perfectly fine, if you choose a career field that pays well and avoids student loan debt. Your passion for art history, history, English literature, or women's studies is meaningless. The world is not going to pay you a good living for your passion, especially when it is a very common passion with a low barrier to entry. If my toilet breaks, I call a plumber. If my roof falls apart, I call a roofer. If my car breaks down, I call a mechanic. If I want to learn about US History, I do not call a "historian-on-demand." I Google it. If you want to get a college degree, it needs to be in a field that provides a true value to other people, not what makes you feel good. Welcome to the "harsh" reality of the world that compensates you for the value you provide to others, not what makes you happy.

What white-collar degrees provide value to society? You have heard it a thousand times: STEM, STEM, STEM. These are jobs that will give you a great income to build your wealth. The more you make, the faster you can build your wealth and the faster you achieve financial freedom. For income generation/wealth building potential, white-collar jobs resulting from a college degree are the best option. They will be challenging to learn, and you will not have as much time to go rage at frat parties, because you will be studying.

But you will be rewarded for four years of hard when you graduate with a comfortable salary and a secure job, while your liberal arts classmates struggle for decades to make a solid living. Degrees to consider include Actuarial Science, Accounting, Chemistry, Computer Science, Management Information Systems, Nursing, Electrical Engineering, and many others. Avoid generic degrees that do not teach an actual skill that do not directly translate into a job, like Business, Business Economics, Management and others. If you see most people avoiding certain degrees because they are "hard," that is the degree to get. This will boost your lifetime earnings, which gives you more opportunity to build wealth. You can study hard for a few years and enjoy financial security for your whole life, or you can take a few easy years upfront to get an easy and spend the rest of your life struggling financially. Your choice.

Now that we have talked about how to increase your income, let us pivot to reducing expenses. Obviously, you need to create a budget. You need to know how much you are making in <u>after</u> tax income, what your monthly expenses are and where they are going. I am not going to go into detail writing down your budget, since there are a thousand and one budget tools you can find with a quick Google search.

The bottom line is you need to take the time to gather your monthly credit card statements and bank statements and write down exactly how much you are spending on each category each month. You should look at them over a three-month period and average out each expense to give you a better picture of how much you are spending for each category each month. If you need help, download Every Dollar app or sign up for Mint.com, which will help you track and classify your expenses digitally.

Once you have your budget written down, you need to divide expenses into non-essential expenses, essential expenses, variable expenses, and fixed expenses. Essential expenses keep you alive and healthy, like food, shelter, health insurance and utilities. Non-essential expenses are expenses you do not need to survive, like Netflix, Spotify, Amazon Prime, going out to eat, alcohol, a sports car payment and more.

Variable expenses are expenses you can reduce or eliminate or remove at the drop a hat, while fixed expenses are contractual obligations that will take you several months or more to change. Your Amazon subscription is a variable expense because you can cancel it at any time; your mortgage is a fixed expense. Sure, you can refinance your mortgage if rates are favorable or sell your home and downsize, but that is not going to happen instantly.

To reduce your expenses in short-term, eliminate as many non-essential and variable expenses as you can. Instead of eating out twice a week, do it once a week or once every two weeks. Evaluate all your subscriptions and cut out ones you do not use. Throw cable out entirely and pay for a much cheaper online streaming service. Drink at home instead of going to the bar. If you use tobacco products, quit. Yes, your lifestyle is going to be reduced, but if you do not have any income right now to save for your financial goals, this is what you must do to get ahead.

If you do not cut expenses, the only option you must maintain your current lifestyle but also increase money available to save is to increase your income. Increasing your income means you are going to have to spend more hours of your finite life making more money to afford your lifestyle. Would you rather work an extra ten hours a week to afford your current lifestyle, or cut out wasteful spending and have more time to yourself? That is your choice, but I know what I would choose. The more frivolous or indulgence expenses you cut in the short-term, the faster you can set yourself up for long term success.

Non-essential and variable expenses can be cut with little effort; essential and fixed expenses can also be reduced but need to be done with more caution and over a longer period. Essential expenses include things like your rent/mortgage, car payment, health insurance, food you eat at home and utilities. You need to evaluate your current lifestyle and determine if you are living above your means. Are you renting a two bed-room apartment but have no kids? Consider moving to a one-bedroom once your lease expires.

Living in a McMansion with five bedrooms, even though you only have two kids? Consider selling and moving into a 3-bedroom once it is financially feasible. Driving around a sports car or a high-end truck? Sell it immediately and buy a much cheaper used car or continue to pay on it but pledge to never get a new car until your current one literally dies.

You should also reevaluate your insurance coverage every year or two to find better rates; you would be surprised what kind of discounts other insurers will offer you for jumping over. If you like to shop at Wegmans or Whole Foods, switch to a cheaper provider like Walmart and buy everything generic. Do whatever it takes to cut your expenses as much as you can; financial freedom will be your reward.

I want to reiterate again why you are going to do this. Consider if you have no savings right now. Are you constantly stressed about money? Does an unexpected expense keep you up at night? Are you planning to never retire because you cannot save a dime? If any of these sounds like you, increasing your income and/or cutting your expenses will eliminate all these concerns. Yes, it is going to suck for a few years as you increase your hours worked and reduce your expenses. You may be jealous of your broke, fake friends who continue to blow their money on meaningless junk that keeps them poor. But the pain and suffering of cutting your lifestyle and working hard will bear fruit in a few short years.

Once you pay off any stupid debts, have a ton of money stashed in a savings account for emergencies and a rapidly growing Roth IRA balance, you will feel better than ever. You'll also be able to budget in more fun money into your budget because you've laid your financial foundation, but this time, you'll be spending money on fun and growing your wealth, while your friends and neighbors are just spending everything they have.

Now that you have decided to graduate from broke loser status, you may be wondering what you are going to do with your newly freed, disposable income. Here is what you are going to do with your cash on a step-by-step basis:

1. <u>Buy a Term Life Insurance Policy</u> – I covered this in the insurance chapter, but you MUST protect your dependents, **if** you have any. And no, I do not sell freaking life insurance. I really believe in term insurance. GET IT.

2. <u>Save one month of ESSENTIAL expenses in an FDIC insured high yield savings account</u> (Synchrony, Ally Bank…Google it for the best current rates). You can do this by selling your stupid sports car and any items in your home you do not use anymore, on top of increasing income/cutting expenses.

3. <u>Get Your Employer 401K Match:</u> Employer 401k matches, if you get them are free money. If you have a 1:1 401K match, you are doubling your money with every dollar contributed up to the match limit. For example, I am a Federal employee. If I contribute 5% of my salary, my total employer match is an additional 5%. I double my money for nothing, simply by contributing to my 401K.

4. <u>Pay off all debt besides your mortgage</u>. Pay the minimum on all your debts except the one you want to pay down first. Attack either the highest interest debt or lowest balance debt with everything you have. Paying off high interest debt first makes financial sense but paying off the lowest balance debt first can give you psychological victories…it is your choice. Throw every spare dollar you have into reducing any debt you have.

5. <u>Increase your emergency fund to 3-6 months of ESSENTIAL expenses</u>. If you have a secure job, rent,

and have no kids, save three months. If you have kids and a home, save six months.

6. <u>Invest</u>. Divert every dime you can to investing. The faster you accumulate wealth, the faster you can retire and the faster you can attain semi or complete financial independence. First, you should already be getting the 401K match at work. After that, fully fund your Roth IRA and your spouse's IRA, if you meet the income thresholds. After that, put as much as you can into your 401K. If you are doing great and plan to retire well before 59.5, you may want to consider purchasing investments in taxable brokerage accounts. You can sell taxable investments at any time and pay taxes; they will not be locked away in a tax advantaged retirement account that will penalize you for early withdrawals.

That is it. My method is like Dave Ramsey's baby-steps, minus paying off your mortgage early and giving to charity. As I explain in the homeownership chapter, it's a dumb idea to pay off you mortgage early unless you have a mortgage rate that is similar to or more than returns you can get investing in stocks. Someone who pays off their mortgage early will miss decades of compounding wealth accumulation in liquid stock mutual funds in exchange for a paid off home. While a paid off home is great, the "wealth" in the home is locked away in equity, which you can only access via a loan or by selling the house; it is highly illiquid. I am not against giving to charity, but I do not consider it an essential step in completing your financial plan.

Once you get to the investing stage, you will start to see significant accumulation of wealth after a few years of CONSISTENTLY buying low cost stock index mutual funds. It is not hard. If you can set up monthly auto withdrawal for your obnoxious $300 cable tv package, you can just as easily set up one to invest for your future. No matter what happens to the market, you keep investing, month in and month out. If you do that, you win. If you do not, you stay broke.

You should also set investment milestones for yourself to motivate you to stick to the plan. $10,000, $50,000, $100,000, and $500,000 are all great milestones to achieve, if you understand it is not going to happen overnight. Once you reach those milestones, you should reward yourself with something nice for a couple hundred bucks. As long as you stick to your investing plan and make it automatic via auto-contributions to your 401K and Roth IRA, you are guaranteed to accumulate way more wealth than the average American loser who blows everything they make because they TV told them to.

Chapter 3: Risk Mitigation

Risk Mitigation is the next step to reforming your terrible financial habits. Risk mitigation is achieved through insurance products that protect your family from financial hardship. Worried about dying prematurely and leaving your family in poverty? You need life insurance. If you still have children living with you, a mortgage, and other debts, and you are the primary breadwinner, you need it. Life insurance is the first thing you will buy before you do anything else. Do not like it? Tough.

Personal finance is not just bought buying stocks. You can either remain a **BROKE LOSER** or take the first step on the path to financial security. Worried you might become totally disabled on the job? You may need disability insurance. Yes, it will cost you some money, but it is a NECESSITY in some scenarios, especially if you are the primary breadwinner. Wondering who will take care of you when you are older? Look into long-term care insurance. Do not screw your kids by forcing them to pay for your long-term care needs because you were too busy blowing your money on shoes to buy a long-term care policy.

NOTE: I do not sell life insurance. I do not get any sort of commission for recommending life insurance. I have zero affiliation with any life insurance company. But I demand you buy a life insurance policy to protect your family; if you refuse to because it's "too expensive" or you have better things to do like buy your fifteenth pistol for your gun collection, then toss this book in the trash. You are a lost cause. If you trust me and decide to buy life insurance, you want term life insurance.

Ignore any scummy salesman who wants to sell whole life, universal life, or any other variant or combination of cash value life insurance. If you contact an agent to buy a term policy and they start talking about a "great investment" or "amazing tax-advantaged benefits," stick your fingers in your ears and repeat "La la la" until they stop. Tell them you are buying term, or you are OUT. Anything other than term is a complete waste of money and will divert dollars from more important things into a terrible product. You want to maximize the amount of money you have for the cash management and investing components of your financial plan.

"Investing" in a whole life or universal life policy will eat up a large part of your disposable income and make it next to impossible to achieve your financial goals. The investment component of your life insurance will also be garbage in comparison to low-cost stock mutual funds. But we will get to that part later.

With term life, you can easily afford to purchase the amount of coverage you need to protect your family for a set period. The term is the cheapest form of life insurance out there because it does not come with any gimmicks or special components. It is insurance in the purest sense. You want the most vanilla, boring term policy you can get for the appropriate amount of time you need it. You die, your family gets a death benefit. It is that simple.

Avoid additions to your policy that increase the cost, also known as "riders." Insurance companies will throw these at you to raise your premium (and their profits) for garbage you will not need. Insurance is a necessary evil that will put a small dent in your monthly savings potential, and you must make every possible effort to keep insurance costs as low as possible. The less you spend on life insurance, the more you can divert as much money as possible to growing your wealth.

Term insurance protects you for a set period. If you die, the insurance company pays a death benefit to your beneficiaries. For example, if you get a $1 million 30-year term policy, you pay a level premium (let us say $40 a month) every month for 30 years. As long you pay that premium on time every month, the policy stays in effect until the expiration date at the end of the 30 year-term. If you die within that 30-year window, your beneficiaries get $1 million. If you do not die, you lose all insurance coverage and stop paying the premium at the 30-year mark. If you want to renew your term insurance after that, your premium cost will skyrocket. But that is irrelevant, because after 30-years you will be self-insured, and you will not need life insurance anymore.

Term insurance protects your family for a fixed period. If you have someone dependent on your income, or if your family would need more money to offset something you are providing to the family free of charge, like being a stay-at-home mom, you need a life insurance policy. When you are young, you will not have enough assets to be self-insured, which means you need to buy life insurance. Self-insured means you have enough assets to fully protect your family without insurance.

Imagine if you had $10 million in the bank and no debt, and your family only needed $2,500 a month to sustain their current standard of living. Would you need life insurance? Nope. Not that you cannot still buy a policy with $10 million in the bank, but your family would not need to depend on it to survive.

If you have a job or watch the kids at home, have a mortgage, car debt and any other debt and you don't have the money set aside to sustain your family indefinitely at their current standard of living, you need enough life insurance to pay all your debt off and support your family at their current standard of living. Think about what would happen if you died without insurance right now. How would your surviving spouse pay the mortgage? How would your family replace the income lost because you died? Even if you are a stay-at-home parent, you need enough life insurance to pay for day care; stay-at-home parents provide real economic benefits that need to be replaced with insurance if the parent dies.

Many insurers will help you determine how much insurance you need, or you can do it yourself. If you decide to have an insurer or agent help you, it's best to do it online so you don't have to deal with a pushy salesman who will try to sell you more garbage that you don't really need. Most websites will ask you a series of questions about your income and lifestyle to determine the amount of coverage required.

A good rule of thumb is your life insurance death benefit should be 10x your annual pre-tax income, but you may need much more than that depending on your debt level and personal circumstances. Just do not scrimp on the amount of insurance just to save money; it is crucial you protect your family. Only broke, selfish losers do not buy adequate life insurance so they can afford to spend money on some other asinine thing, like a new fishing pool or their daily dipping tobacco habit.

You may have life insurance through your employer, but it probably will not be enough to cover your needs. You should shop around for the best insurance rates, with a minimum of three quotes from different insurers to get the best deal possible. Www.policygenius.com is a great resource to compare different insurance quotes, or you can go directly to each insurer to get a quote.

I will remind you again. ONLY GET TERM INSURANCE. You will not need insurance coverage your entire life. Your mortgage will be paid off after 30 years. Your children will get through college and move out of the house. Your retirement nest egg will grow to the point where your spouse can live off the balance alone, even without your income. Term can cover you for 30 years, which is ample time to pay off your mortgage and get your kids out of the house. Term is between 10-15x cheaper than whole life insurance, which frees up more money for you to invest for your retirement and other life goals. Would you rather pay $60 a month for $1 million in coverage, or $600 a month?

Thought so. Do not get sucked in by scummy insurance salesman who will try to convince you it is a great idea to pair investing with insurance. Any money you put into a life insurance product that is not directly correlated with the cost of insurance can generate higher returns through your own investing. Life insurance agents are just out to make a fat commission of your ignorance. Investing is investing, insurance is insurance; keep them separate.

If you apply for a large life insurance policy, you are probably going to have to do a medical exam. Companies will issue some policies without a medical exam under a certain amount of death benefit coverage, but the policy will most likely not be enough to fully protect your family. For larger policies, generally over $500,000 in death benefit, the insurance company wants to understand how healthy you are before they issue you a policy and risk millions of dollars.[6]

These exams consist of a qualified medical professional taking your height, weight, blood pressure, a blood sample and a urine sample. You will answer a laundry list of questions about your current medical conditions and lifestyle. The insurer will want to know if you sky dive, fly single engine airplanes, scuba dive and many other things

---

[6] https://www.trustedchoice.com/life-insurance/coverage-types/no-medical-exam/

about you. They will want to know about your parent's health, any medical conditions they may have and other family history.

The medical exam and questions may seem invasive and like overkill, but it makes sense. The insurer is taking on the risk of paying out hundreds of thousands or millions of dollars to your family if you die over the policy term. Insurers are in the business of making money and want to mitigate as much risk as possible by understanding your current and potential future medical problems. Do not lie on your application; if you do, your family's death benefit may be considerably reduced. That is also called fraud.

Based on your medical exam, the insurer will offer you a policy for a certain monthly cost, or premium. Your premium is generally lower the younger and healthier you are and will vary by insurance company. If you get married, start a family or have anyone dependent on your income, you want to get a policy as soon as possible. Do not wait until you are old, fat and potentially uninsurable before you consider a policy. The insurance company is not obligated to insure you and can reject your application altogether, depending on how risky you are.

Once you purchase your life insurance policy, which you will do TODAY because you have made the decision to break free of the **BROKE LOSER** mentality, your next consideration will be disability insurance. Disability insurance replaces a portion of your income if something happens to you and you cannot work. Disability insurance is not Workers Compensation, or Workers Comp, although it serves a similar purpose. Worker's Comp laws are different in each state, but they will generally replace a portion of your income, usually 66%, if you are injured <u>at work</u> and cannot perform your job anymore. If you are injured outside of work, you are not going to receive Worker's Comp.

Your Worker's Comp may also have a finite payment period. That is where disability insurance steps in. Disability insurance will replace a portion of your income if you become unable to work due to injury or illness, regardless of whether you are on the job or not. How much income replaced is based on how much you specific in your policy; the more income you want covered, the more you are going to pay.

Disability insurance can be either short term or long term. You do not need short-term disability insurance if you follow my advice and have some emergency savings set aside to cover several months of essential expenses. Like life insurance, you can be self-insured from short term disability if you have enough money; this allows you to skip overpaying for premiums you do not need and investing them in assets instead.

Disability insurance should cover the income you need to keep your family afloat if you lose your job. Your monthly essential bills, like your rent/mortgage, food, utilities, and health insurance should be covered by your disability insurance. Your Netflix or tanning subscription do not fall into the category of essential bills. You can budget in non-essentials, but you are going to pay more in premiums if you do. Which you do not want to do, because you want as much money going toward assets that will generate you more money in the future. Disability insurance is a necessary evil, but you want to minimize your payments, so you only are paying for what you need to survive.

You should also check with your employer to see if they already have you enrolled in a disability insurance plan as part of your employment benefits. While you may have some coverage through your employer, it may not be enough to meet your needs. You need to do your research and buy a policy through a private insurer if you need more coverage. If you are not sure about all the considerations for disability insurance, call up a larger insurance career and talk with an agent. Just do not go meet one of them in person. It is a lot easier to say "no" to somebody over the phone if you think they are selling you a load of BS than it is to say to someone face to face. Most people buy products they do not need because they are pushed into them by pushy salesmen. If you determine you need a supplemental long-term disability policy from the private sector, make room in your budget and buy it. If you do not, you could wind up permanently disabled and broke. Disability can happen to any of us when we least expect it, and it can easily derail even the best laid financial plans.

You may think you don't need long-term disability insurance, since you can count on good ol' Social Security Disability Insurance (SSDI) to swoop in and save the day. That is just plain dumb. The average wait time to get a hearing to qualify for SSDI is 538 days[7]. Imagine waiting over a year to qualify for disability benefits when you have a reduced income coming in, or no income at. You would be screwed.

On top of that, SSDI claims are rejected 53% of the time. That is straight from the Social Security Administration

---

[7] https://www.globenewswire.com/news-release/2019/02/12/1720954/0/en/More-Than-800-000-Waiting-for-Social-Security-Disability-Hearings-Wait-Times-Are-Declining-But-Still-Average-18-Months.html#:~:text=12%2C%202019%20(GLOBE%20NEWSWIRE),ranking%20of%20the%20hearing%20backlog.

itself.[8] So if you plan to rely on SSDI, you are resting your hopes on a ridiculously long wait-time and a 50/50 chance your claim will pass scrutiny. Compare that to long term disability insurance, which has an average waiting period of 90 days before it begins to pay out of benefits.[9]

Long-term disability insurance also covers a much higher percentage of your income than SSDI and is much more likely to be approved. On average, long-term disability insurance replaces 60% of your income, while SSDI only pays an average of $1,197 per month. Long-term disability will keep you from living the rest of your life in abject poverty. Want to avoid the risk of lifetime poverty and begging Social Security to give you a small pittance to survive? Pay 1-3% of your income for a long-term disability policy. Check out www.policygenius.com do get a quick estimate of how different levels of coverage would cost you.

Long term care (LTC) insurance is the final consideration for your risk mitigation strategy, but only when you or your parents are in your late 50s or beyond. A LTC policy is a wealth preservation insurance policy that will mitigate the risk you drain your life's savings on long-term care expenses. This applies to both you and your parents. If

---

[8] https://www.ssa.gov/policy/docs/statcomps/di_asr/2011/sect04.html
[9] https://www.policygenius.com/disability-insurance/disability-insurance-elimination-periods/

you do not have a policy, consider getting one. If your parents are getting older and do not have much money, you want to discuss getting a policy with them. A LTC policy could save you from being a blood-sucking burden on your children and grandchildren if you do not have any wealth accumulated for retirement.

One of the most selfish, <u>disgusting</u> things a person can do is live irresponsibly their whole life by not saving money, deciding not to purchase a LTC policy because "I can't afford my cruises if I pay the premium," and then becoming a financial burden to their children when they become old and can't support themselves. An elderly parent who has no money, no LTC insurance plan and becomes too old to care for themselves will cost their children untold thousands of dollars to support them, not to mention the stress the children have to go through to re-orient their lives around their helpless parent.

Elderly parents will not only drain their children's financial future, but their grandchildren's as well. Mommy and daddy will have to cut college savings for their children because grandpa blew all his money when he was younger and did not have the foresight to purchase a long-term case policy. If you are in your 50s and reading this, you need to do your research on LTC. If you are in your 20s and 30s and your parents are in their 50s or 60s, you need to sit down with them and talk about their long-term care plan. You may be surprised to find out your parent's plan long-term plan is to be an intergenerational vampire. If that is the case, act now to prevent that from happening.

Long-term care insurance is "designed to cover long-term services and supports, including personal and custodial care in a variety of settings such as your home, a community organization, or other facility." [10] The average annual cost of a policy in the United States is $2,727, but may be much higher or lower depending on your age and health.[11] If you get old and become unable to perform at least two activities of daily living (ADLs) (bathing, dressing, eating)[12], an LTC policy will provide you a daily benefit up to a certain amount to defray the cost of assisted care at a nursing home, assisted living facility or for in-home care.

For example, you may buy a policy that covers you for five years of assisted living expenses up to a maximum of

---

[10] https://longtermcare.acl.gov/costs-how-to-pay/what-is-long-term-care-insurance/index.html

[11] https://www.daveramsey.com/blog/who-needs-long-term-care-insurance#:~:text=According%20to%20a%20LifePlans%2C%20Inc,(four%20is%20most%20common).

[12] https://longtermcare.acl.gov/costs-how-to-pay/what-is-long-term-care-insurance/index.html

$200 per day. The premium for your policy will vary depending on your age and health when you purchase it, the daily amount your policy will cover for your healthcare, how many years the policy will pay out for and many other factors. Basically, the more risk you are to the insurance company, the higher the premium they will charge you. For example, women tend to live longer than men, so generally expect a woman's LTC premium to be higher than a man.

You do not need to buy a policy in your 30s or 40s; your decision to purchase an LTC can be put off to your late 50s or early 60s. Once you get into your 50s and early 60s, you'll need to decide quickly whether you need a policy or not, because every year that goes by will increase the premium you have to pay. It will also increase the likelihood you will develop a health condition that will make you uninsurable and putting your family at risk for huge financial losses. Your main consideration when looking at an LTC policy is your wealth accumulation by your late 50s.

If you have been diligent with your investing, you may have several million dollars saved for retirement. With that much wealth, your risk of depleting your retirement savings to pay for LTC is low. In that case, LTC is not a requirement, but still an option if you want to guarantee you pass on a significant percentage of your wealth to your heirs.

If you only have a few hundred thousand dollars to your name, it will be a 50/50 proposition. If you have nothing saved for retirement because you blew all your money on BS, it becomes a necessity.

How much could skipping over a LTC insurance policy cost you? On average, a person alive at age 65 years or older will have a 50/50 chance of needing LTC. If they are uninsured, they will pay an average of $140,000 out of pocket. 13% of people who use some form of assisted care will need LTC care for five years or more, while 48% will need LTC for 1 year or less. 63% of people will not spend a dime on assisted living their whole lives, while 9% will spend over $250,000. Overall, one in four people will spend more than $40,000 in LTC costs.[13]

What does this all mean? As I said previously, if you or your parents have nothing saved for retirement, you need to purchase a long-term care policy. There is a better than even chance that your parents will not need to use a LTC policy at all, but if it does happen and your parents are broke, you are in trouble. If you don't, you may have to upend or your life and drain your savings to support your financially irresponsible parent, or you'll drain your own children for the

---

[13] https://www.aarp.org/caregiving/financial-legal/info-2018/long-term-care-insurance-fd.html

same reason if you need assisted living later in life. If you have a retirement nest egg in the millions, you are self-insured and will be better off investing the premiums instead.

Think Medicare or Medicaid will save you? Think again. Medicare will only pay a portion of skilled nursing facility costs for the first 100 days of hospital admission, after which you are on the hook. You will not be reimbursed for long-term custodial care, or care that does not require skilled care such as "skilled nursing services, physical therapy, or other types of therapy."[14] Basically, Medicare will pay for temporary, skilled medical services, but they aren't going to pay for a caretaker to come to your house every day for the next five years and empty your waste-bin and help you get dressed.

Medicaid will pay for long-term care services, but to qualify you will need to have no wealth and have an extremely low income. For example, in 2019 "the income limit is set at $2,313 per month and the asset limits at $2,000 for an individual" to qualify for Medicaid's Long-Term Services and Supports (LTSS).[15] Unless your long term plan

---

[14] https://longtermcare.acl.gov/medicare-medicaid-more/medicare.html#:~:text=Medicare%20covers%20medically%20necessary%20care,referred%20to%20as%20custodial%20care).
[15] https://www.verywellhealth.com/your-assets-magi-and-medicaid-eligibility-

is to have a crap income in retirement and have no retirement savings whatsoever, you're not going to qualify for Medicaid. That program is designed for people who are in desperate poverty and truly need the government support. Do not be a piece of scum and try to manipulate the system by gifting away all your wealth to your family just so you can qualify for Medicaid.

Risk mitigation is an important part of your financial well-being. Insurance is a necessary evil that you can eventually phase out of your budget once you accumulate enough assets to self-insure. Unfortunately, most people will not accumulate significant assets to self-insure until they have diligently invested in assets for decades. In the interim, you must protect yourself with insurance. When you are forced to spend money on a liability, i.e. insurance, you want to find the best value for your money. This frees up as much income as possible to invest in assets without leaving yourself open to a huge financial loss.

Term-life insurance is the best value for your money; it provides all the protection you need at the lowest cost. Long-term disability insurance will protect your family from a loss of income during your working years until you have

---

4144975#:~:text=Most%20of%20the%20government%20programs,at%20%242%2C000%20for%20an%20individual.

acquired enough wealth to support yourself without working. Long-term care insurance protects you from draining a portion or all your accumulated life's savings when you cannot take of yourself anymore. It also protects your children and grandchildren from having to foot the bill for your long-term care if you do not have any assets; this stops you from draining your descendants like an inter-generational vampire.

Chapter 4: Investing

They call me Mr. Bugatti. I day trade stocks, bro. I am a financial professional who can predict changes in the market before anyone else; I'm going to make it huge one day. I do tons of research on individual stocks, like reading opinion pieces Google News Business articles. It is not that hard to beat the market, you just gotta analyze charts and read an article or two, you know? You just gotta be smarter than the average investor, who is so dumb they buy index funds that track the market. Pfft. Index funds never beat the market because they ARE the market.

Why would you want to just achieve boring returns at just the market rate? That is dumb. You got to be in it to win it. It is totally worth it to risk your entire life savings two or three stock bets, bro. If you do not, you are a loser. Yea, I lost 50% of my portfolio after the COVID-19 drop, but that is just a temporary loss. I got a new HOT STOCK TIP from Reddit that's gonna make me 10,000% returns in one year. I am putting the rest of my money in that stock. Get on the bandwagon, you unsophisticated loser. Later.

Do not be Mr. Bugatti. Mr. Bugatti is a **BROKE LOSER** who thinks he can Get-Rich-Quick because he saw "HOT STOCK TIPS, BRO" on a Reddit forum. People like him scare the average person away from investing in stocks because they are often the subject of stories about people "losing it all" in the market. Losing it all in the stock market does happen, but only for people who do not diversify their investments. Investing in stocks is easy if you have a long-term mindset and you automatically invest a part of your paycheck every month in a diversified stock index mutual fund. I firmly believe stock investing is the optimum way for the average American to achieve wealth. You just need to know WHAT you are investing in and WHY are you are investing in it.

The average American sucks at investing and does not even know what investing means. The average stock "investor" resembles Mr. Bugatti and others like him who gamble in the market and make investing seem difficult and complex; its' not. Write people like Mr. Bugatti off, because speculators like him are "spraying and praying" their money into overhyped stocks that they read about in a newspaper or saw on YouTube.

The key to investing success with stocks is all about reigning in bad behaviors, exercising self-control, good self-discipline and understanding short term fluctuations in the market are based on emotion and hype. Investing takes patience and a long-term outlook. You are not going to get rich quickly. I say again, YOU ARE NOT GOING TO GET RICH QUICKLY. If you have a get-rich-quick mentality, you are lazy and will not succeed in your investing endeavors. There is nothing out there that will make you extremely rich very quickly unless you have immeasurable luck, which 99.99999% of people will not have. Some are lucky and win the lottery. Others receive a surprise inheritance. That is not going to be you. Buying lottery tickets is a guaranteed way to lose money.

Most American's are pitifully broke, which means you probably will not get a large inheritance. Accept the fact you must sacrifice and work hard over decades to achieve financial success. If you cannot accept this because you are short-sighted, lazy, or have a victim complex, enjoy being a **BROKE LOSER** for the rest of your life.

Wealth is the real indicator of success in America, not your income. Wealth is attained not by waiting for mommy and daddy to die or by collecting a welfare check from the government, but from increasing your income, reducing your expenses and sustained investment. Let us define investing. Investing is <u>deferring</u> gratification in the present to achieve a financial goal sometime in the future. It is that easy. Paying for college, a home down payment, funding your retirement accounts, saving for a vacation. All of these are financial goals that can be achieved through investment.

When you buy assets, you are investing. As I will reiterate many times in this book, I am a CPA (*respect me*) and know what an asset is it in an accounting sense. An accounting asset is not the same as a personal finance asset. In accounting, everything you own is an asset, even if it loses value over time and costs your money. A personal finance asset has an upfront cost but pays you back every month/quarter/yearly and/or increases in value over time. Buying a car is not an investment and it is not an asset in personal finance. Cars cost you money every month and lose value quickly after you purchase them.

The home you live in is not an asset or investment. Homes do generally increase in value but cost you tens of thousands of dollars a year in mortgage interest, property taxes, HOA dues, homeowners insurance, maintenance, and more. The home you live in does not PAY you; you pay it. A home you rent to tenants IS an asset if it generates a positive cash flow. A good stock mutual fund that pays yearly dividends and appreciates in value IS an investment. Get it? If you buy something that pays you, it is an asset. If you buy something and you pay it, it is a liability.

How do you get the money to buy assets as investments? We already covered this in the Cash Management chapter, but in summary, you must make as much money as you possibly can and cut out as much spending as you can. Do you want to have $2 million retirement nest egg when you are 60, but you spend all your money on "experiences" and "living your life" while working a minimum wage job? It is not going to happen.

Want to make a good income so you can invest your money and build wealth, but you choose to get a liberal arts degree and move to an expensive liberal mega-city to hopefully make it big in the Social Media Marketing Manager industry? It is probably not going to happen. The amount of wealth you build is directly proportional to how much-unallocated income you make for yourself every month. Unallocated income is simply how much you make after-tax every month, minus how you must you spend on liabilities. The remainder is cash you have to buy investments with.

The more unallocated income you have, the more you can invest and faster you build wealth. Unallocated income also has a multiplier effect and grows exponentially, because your investments increase your unallocated income, which then you re-invest back into your investments.

The assets that give you any shot at attaining wealth are stocks, real estate, or starting your own business. I personally recommend stock index fund investing with a long-term mindset as the optimum way to build wealth for the average American that does not have much money to work with when they start their investing journey. Real estate and business are other viable alternatives once you have accumulated some capital, but they require more hustle and are much riskier.

On an average income, stock index fund investing will make you a few million dollars over a lifetime. If you want more than that, you need to consider real estate and a business venture. Real estate investing and business ventures are much riskier and more difficult to pull off than stock investing, but they can make you exceeding wealthy if you claw your way to success and you have the grit to hustle and work long hours on top of your regular job.

Just know that only 30% of businesses survive their 10th year and will most likely destroy your work-life balance for decades until you are big enough to afford your own management.[16] That's the price you pay to potentially become a multi-multi-millionaire or billionaire.

I personally do not like the hassle and risks associated with real estate investing (stupid tenants, repairs, debt, etc....) and accept I will never be mega-rich because of it. Doing real estate investing on your own is also fraught with risks, is horribly illiquid, and is not diversified. If you buy one or two properties in your local community and pour the majority of your investable dollars into them, you're hinging your investing success on one or two properties, in one town, in one state, in one country.

You could miscalculate and make a bad investment in a property that does not produce your expected monthly cash flow, needs more repairs than you expected or experience terrible tenants that trash your property. You're also open to employer risk; if your town depends on one or two major employers and they close up shop, you'll quickly find your properties will plummet in value as people lose their jobs and move out of town.

I do not recommend the average person invest in their own real estate ventures; instead, you can invest in a real

---

[16] https://www.fundera.com/blog/what-percentage-of-small-businesses-fail#:~:text=The%20fast%20answer%20for%20what,many%20American%20small%20businesses%20survive.

estate investment trust (REIT) and be exposed to thousands or tens of thousands of properties in multiple states, countries and industries. That is TRUE diversification.

However, I do understand that reaching a net worth in the $100s of millions or billions requires an inordinate level of blood, sweat and tears that I do not want to give. You need to decide how much risk you are willing to accept over your lifetime. I personally do not want to hinge my life's savings on a few investment properties in a small corner of the globe, which is why I do not invest in any rental properties. Communist **BROKE LOSERS** will have you believe millionaires do not work hard and inherit their money with little effort, but that is patently false.

88% of millionaires are self-made.[17] EIGHTY-EIGHT PERCENT. If you are envious of a successful real estate investor or business owner because they put in the extra effort needed to get where they are, then you are a just whiny, **BROKE, JEALOUS LOSER**. If you are envious of people who have more money than you because they invested their money properly and worked hard to achieve it, you are a **BROKE LOSER**. If you want to become a real estate

---

[17] https://money.usnews.com/money/blogs/on-retirement/articles/7-myths-about-millionaires#:~:text=A%202017%20survey%20from%20Fidelity,of%20millionaires%20are%20self%2Dmade.

investor or business owner, pick up another book. If you want to achieve wealth through investing in stocks, read on.

Stocks are the key to financial success and are not risky in the long term if you are not irresponsible with your money. Stock market returns crush inflation over the long run through stock price appreciation and dividend reinvestment. Stocks as an aggregate may have a bad year or decade, but over the course of a lifetime they always come through for investors who control their emotions and buy and hold stocks for the long run.

You need to be heavily invested in stocks in your 20s-50s (90%+) and have a roughly 50/50 split of bonds and stocks by the time you retire in your sixties if that is your goal. If you fear stocks because they fluctuate rapidly in the short term, you are always going to be broke. Stocks are easy to understand once they are demystified by a sexy, highly educated teacher like myself.

A stock represents ownership in a company. When you own stock in a company, you own a small piece of that company. If a new company needs money to scale up their enterprise and they do not want to go into more debt, they will either seek venture capital funding or "go public" and issue stock in exchange for a large cash infusion from investors. A company issues stock to be traded on stock exchanges around the world through large sales called initial public offerings (IPOs). After the IPO, the company gets the cash they need to grow their business in exchange for giving up ownership of a portion of the company to investors.

The company can use the investor's cash to grow their business, hopefully making the company more valuable and profitable in the long run. Investors will buy these stocks because they believe the stock price will appreciate over time. Investors also hope to eventually get dividend payments from the company, which are distributions of the company's profits to stockholders. Stockholders get other benefits, such the right to vote in the board of directors or designate a proxy to do so on their behalf. They also take on risk they lose their entire investment if the company goes out of business; stock ownership is not a free lunch.

After an IPO, a stock will be listed on a stock exchange. A stock exchange is a place where stocks are exchanged between buyers and sellers. It is in the name. There are several stock exchanges in the United States, like the New York Stock Exchange (NYSE) and the NASDAQ (National Association of Securities Dealers Automated Quotations). There are roughly 2,800 stocks actively traded on the NYSE and 3,300 traded on the NASDAQ. There are also dozens of stock exchanges around the world, like the

Tokyo Stock Exchange, the London Stock Exchange and the Shanghai Stock Exchange.

There is not one "stock market," and you can only buy certain stocks on one or maybe two stock exchanges. There are dozens of stock markets around the world, and they are radically different from each other because the amount and type of companies listed on them are completely different. For example, you can only buy Apple stock through the NASDAQ and you can only buy General Motors stock on the NYSE. Most companies choose to only list their stock on one stock exchange for liquidity reasons, but you will occasionally find dual-listed stocks as well.

If you hear on the news the stock market is crashing, that does not mean every stock around the world is dropping in value. The "stock market" is not a single monolithic entity but is composed of thousands of stocks traded on dozens of exchanges around the world. The NYSE could see an overall decrease in value in one day, but that does not mean every stock listed on the NYSE is decreasing in value. It is not uncommon for a few stocks on an exchange to rocket up in value when most stocks on the exchange are crashing. During any economic crisis, some companies will become more valuable while others will lose value. For example, the 2019-2020 Coronavirus pandemic. Airline and cruise stocks were crushed during the pandemic because travel and leisure dropped to a standstill, but companies like Clorox Co. rocketed up in value.

Why? Sales of cleaning supplies and disinfectants skyrocketed during the pandemic, translating to revenue and profitability growth for Clorox and others. Do not ever think every company across the world is losing value during an economic crisis, because you will always be wrong.

So how to do people get a sense of whether stock markets around the world are going up and down? How do you know which industries are doing well and which are not? That is where indices step in. A market index is simply a way to track the overall performance of a basket of stocks. A market index will have a basket of stocks and expresses the overall change in value of that basket of stocks through one number. You can have one index that tracks the overall performance of every stock listed in NYSE and another that tracks the NASDAQ.

There are indices that track only small companies, medium sized companies, large companies, US Markets, Foreign Stock Markets, the health care sector, the consumer discretionary sector and more. Basically, every type of stock classification you can imagine likely has an index associated with it. The indices most people see on the news every day are the Dow Jones Industrial Average (DJI), the S&P 500 (INX) and the NASDAQ Composite (IXIC). You may not know this, but the Dow Jones only tracks the movement of 30 large US stocks, the S&P 500 tracks 505 medium-large US Stocks, while the NASDAQ Composite tracks all 3,300 stocks listed on the NASDAQ. Each index is designed to track a certain section of the market.

Why do we care about indices? Because you need to know what you are looking at when you see the "stock market" crashing on the news. You also need to know that indices are created and periodically adjusted by large institutions like Standard & Poor's, Wilshire Associates, Morgan Stanley and others, and while they may be great indicators of the overall performance of the market, they still involve human judgement in their design and maintenance. When you are shopping for mutual funds, you need to know they are either trying to track an index or beat the index most associated with their investment strategy.

If you only buy and sell large US companies in your brokerage account, you goal is to beat the S&P500 over time. If you want to buy a large cap US stock mutual fund, you want that mutual fund to beat the index (or simply track it with an index fund). Since the S&P500 represents large US Companies which account for over 80% of the US market capitalization, it serves as a great benchmark to help investors in large companies' gauge how they are doing compared to the market.

You can either trade your own stocks in a brokerage account or buy stock mutual funds. I do not recommend you buy and sell individual stocks unless you do so as speculative investments with a very small percentage of your portfolio. First, it is much harder for a retail investor to buy a diversified stock portfolio with just a few thousand dollars than it is for a stock mutual fund with billions of dollars in investable assets. With only a few thousand dollars at your disposal, you may only be able to buy stock in three or four companies, exposing your entire portfolio to the fortunes of just a few stocks.

You can buy fractional shares to create a diverse portfolio, but if you do that, you will be constantly busy rebalancing your portfolio. Retail investors also suck horribly at beating the market because the liquidity of stocks and the inability to control their emotions leads them to make bad financial decisions.[18] Between 1995-2015, S&P 500 index returned an annualized 9.85% per year while the

---

[18] https://www.forbes.com/sites/advisor/2014/04/24/why-the-average-investors-investment-return-is-so-low/#2a987dbe111a

average stock investor only returned 5.19% per year. [19] The bottom line? Unless you are uncharacteristically disciplined and able to separate your emotions from stock trading, you will not, under ANY circumstances, hold individual stocks as a major portion of your portfolio. You WILL buy mutual funds. If you do not, have fun being a **BROKE LOSER** for the rest of your life.

What is a mutual fund? A mutual fund is a way for investors to pool their cash and hand it off to a small investment team to buy investments on their behalf. Investors pay a team of professionals to invest their money for them according to their investment objectives. Mutual funds are offered by several different investment management companies like Vanguard, Fidelity, Charles Schwab and others will hire a group of investment professionals to manage a specific portfolio for their clients. These investment professionals, called fund managers, will take charge of a mutual fund with a specific investment purpose.

Hundreds, thousands or even millions of investors will buy a share of the mutual fund with cash. The fund managers will use this cash to buy investments consistent

---

[19] https://www.thebalance.com/why-average-investors-earn-below-average-market-returns-2388519

with the fund's objectives. Mutual funds can be composed entirely of bonds, stocks, a blend of the two, real estate investment trusts and more.

Mutual funds eliminate the "risk" of investing in stocks in the long run, if you buy the right ones. The biggest risk to any investor's success is their emotions. Diversified stock index mutual funds are NOT risky when you look at their performance over decades, but investors ignore hard evidence and buy and sell their investments based purely on emotions. Mutual funds mitigate, but do not eliminate, the risk an investor will sell their stock holdings on an emotional whim. An investor can still be dumb and decide to sell their mutual fund shares when the mutual fund share prices drops in value due to a recession or some other event, which is the worst time to sell.

But it's much less likely to happen because, while you can trade individual stocks throughout the day from market open to close, mutual fund shares can only be bought and sold at the end of the business day after markets shut down. Mutual funds also have a specific objective they are designed to meet or asset class they are supposed to invest in. When an investor wants to buy and track a large-cap US Stock index, they can buy an S&P 500 mutual fund. That fund will track the S&P 500 index no matter what, while the investor, had they decided to trade individual stocks instead, may be tempted to deviate into another asset class and break from their core portfolio position based on temporary market conditions. Mutual funds help you stay the course.

What stock mutual funds should you buy? First, you will only buy index funds; do not consider, for even one second, buying an actively managed fund. Over the past ten years, less than 10% of actively managed large cap US stock mutual funds beat their associated index. While index funds may not be the end-all-be-all for every asset class, if you're mostly investing in stocks, index funds are the way to go.[20] Once you listen to my advice and invest in an index fund, you must understand you will never beat the return of the index the fund tracks because you are effectively buying the index. But that is okay, because even the professionals who actively try to beat the index fail most of the time.

Index funds have certain advantages that actively managed funds cannot compete with, which drags down the performance of actively managed mutual funds. Index funds charge extremely low fees to investors because managers are not providing a special service or promising to provide superior returns; all they do is buy the stocks in the index.

---

[20] https://www.marketwatch.com/story/more-evidence-that-passive-fund-management-beats-active-2019-09-12

Actively managed funds charge higher fees to compensate the fund managers for their expertise and for the cost of doing market research to find the best investments for their fund. Index funds also have little investment turnover and tax expenses because they are not constantly buying and selling winning and losing stocks.

Actively managed funds not only have to beat the index they are competing against but also fight the return-reducing effect of taxation. Active funds also tend to have higher cash balances for various reasons, which drags down long term returns over time. When you factor in the cost of actively managed fund fees, taxes, cash balances and turnover, you quickly see that even if an actively managed fund outperforms an index, they still fall behind when you factor in all expenses. This has held true for decades, and I don't see actively managed funds ever beating index funds; the inherent costs associated with active management are just too crippling to overcome.

Large Cap US Stock index funds I recommend are any funds that track the S&P 500 and the NASDAQ Composite indices. Large Cap stocks are large, stable companies that have a market capitalization of $10 billion or more. They still have room to grow in value over time and they tend to pay a stable or increasing dividend. The S&P

500 is a popular Large-Cap stock index that accounts for 70-80% of the entire market capitalization of the entire US Stock market and is well diversified amongst different sectors. When you buy the S&P 500, you are buying a small percentage all of US Companies, but these companies are huge and as a whole dwarf the rest of the companies in the US in market capitalization. The S&P500 index tracks companies on both the NYSE and NASDAQ, while the NASDAQ Composite index only tracks stocks listed on the NASDAQ exchange. Because of this, you will see some overlap.

The NASDAQ composite also accounts for a huge percentage of the total US Stock market's capitalization but is more heavily weighted toward technology stocks than the S&P 500. They also have significant overlap in the stock's they track, but the weight of each stock on the index is calculated differently. For example, the S&P 500 might only have Apple stock count as 5% of its in value, while the Nasdaq might have Apple count for 8% of its total value.

You can find S&P 500 and/or Nasdaq Composite at any number of investment brokers like Vanguard and Fidelity. Vanguard typically has a $3,000 investment minimum while Fidelity has $0 minimums; you need to shop around to find what broker is best for you. But for the love of God, do not pay any sales charges or high management fees for an index fund, which is anything above 0.2% of assets managed.[21]

US Middle and small capitalization stocks are another great long-term investment. Mid-Cap stocks have a market capitalization between $2-$10 billion, while small caps have $2 billion or less. Small-cap stocks have much more growth potential than large caps, but also have a higher likelihood of failing because they are small companies. They usually do not pay dividends.

Mid-Cap stocks are a happy medium between Large-Caps and Small-Caps, with higher growth potential than large caps and a lower likelihood to fail than small-caps. If you want to invest in US Mid-Cap stock index funds, look for funds that track the S&P Midcap 400 Index, the CRSP US Mid Cap Index or the Russell Midcap Index. For small caps, look for index funds that track the S&P SmallCap 600, CRSP U.S. Small Cap, MSCI USA Small Cap, or Dow Jones U.S. Small Cap indexes.[22]

---

[21] https://www.investopedia.com/ask/answers/032715/when-expense-ratio-considered-high-and-when-it-considered-low.asp#:~:text=The%20average%20expense%20ratio%20for,typical%20ratio%20is%20about%200.2%25.

[22] https://www.morningstar.com/articles/935655/the-most-popular-small-cap-index-isnt-the-best

Is all this overwhelming? Are there so many options that you just do not know where to start? <u>Here is all you must do</u>. Go to Vanguard or Fidelity.com. RIGHT NOW. Open a Roth IRA or brokerage account if you have already maxed your Roth for the year. Filter out everything except Target Retirement index funds and pick the one that most closely matches the year you want to retire. Click "Buy" once you click on your target date mutual fund. Set up automatic investments every month, not to exceed $500 a month so you do not overcontribute to your IRA and get penalized. That is it. You are now investing for your future. Too much work for you? Got to go watch the Kardashians instead? Enjoy being a **BROKE LOSER** for the rest of your life.

Why a Target Retirement Index fund that matches your retirement date in a Roth IRA? Target Retirement funds are fire and forget, all-in-one investments. A Target Retirement fund is a mutual fund that invests in other mutual funds and has a target retirement date, usually in the title. The target retirement date is the day the investor wants to retire. For example, if you are 30 years old in 2020 and want to retire at 60, you would invest in a 2050 Target Retirement Fund. The mutual funds within the Target Retirement fund will be index funds that track broad market indices that give investors broad exposure to domestic and international stock and bond markets.

As you approach your retirement date, the target retirement fund will reduce the percent of your portfolio allocate in "risky" assets like stocks into "safer" assets like bonds. For example, if you buy a 2050 Target-Retirement Fund in 2020, the fund will have something like 80-90% of its invested in stocks divided between funds like a Total US Stock Market Index fund and a Total International Stock Market fund, and 10-20% in US and International bonds. By 2040, the fund may have a 60/40 stock/bond allocation and 50/50 stocks/bonds in 2050. As time goes on, the fund transitions from building wealth with stocks to preserving wealth with bonds.

I recommend Fidelity or Vanguard Target Retirement funds; they expose you the entire world's stock and bond markets through broadly diversified stock and bond index funds. It is just too easy. If you are a new investor and you have no clue what you are doing, this is the BEST way to invest your money, hands down, no holds barred. Anyone that tells your otherwise is a clown who does not have your best interests at heart.

I also recommend you invest in index funds because they are very low cost and tax efficient. Actively managed funds require more overhead because the fund managers are expending time and money to research and pick the stocks or bonds, they think will make the most money in their defined investment market. These extra costs are passed on to the investor.

Active managers are also buying and selling stocks more often as they modify their positions to take advantage of market opportunities; this increases the fund's overall taxes owed and brokerage costs, which are passed on to the investors. Conversely, an index fund manager's only job is to replicate the performance of a pre-determined basket of stocks or bonds (or both) called an index. There is not much thought that goes into running an index fund; you make sure the funds' investments track the desired benchmark accurately and you let it ride. You do not need to incur expenses doing research because you are not trying to beat the market; you are tracking the market itself.

This also leads to reduced turnover, or transaction costs and taxes. While you may think indices are boring and only guarantee you the returns of the overall market, the simple fact is that active managers have consistently failed to beat their benchmark index when your account for transaction costs and investment fees. Indexes are the way to go, at least until active managers can start consistently beating the market when factoring in active management's increased costs.

Finally, we will go into more detail about Roth IRAs later in the book, but for this section, IRAs are a great way, tax efficient way to invest your money. When you initially purchase a Target Retirement index fund in your Roth IRA, you will never have to worry about paying taxes on it again if you do not break any rules. The beauty of this tax-free investment is that while your money is growing over time in the Target Retirement Fund, you can continue to educate yourself on responsible and intelligent long-term investment strategies.

If you determine that you actually don't like the asset allocation of the Target Retirement fund, you can sell the fund inside the Roth and buy different mutual funds that better fit your desired asset allocation strategy. Since the money is invested inside the Roth, you will pay **zero** taxes to sell your Target Retirement fund at a gain and invest in new funds. If you did the same thing outside an IRA, you would get a hefty tax bill if you sold your Target Retirement fund at a gain and bought new funds; you don't want to do that, because taxes are toxic to your retirement goals.

If you are still getting cold feet about starting to invest, think about this; hesitation is the number one killer of wealth building. The average American grows up with broke parents and will stay broke their entire life because they never take the big step and _**buy**_ a mutual fund. They blow every dime they make on useless items and for short-term pleasures. I guess it is just too hard for the average American to click some buttons and transfer money into mutual funds; they must be too busy refreshing their Facebook feed or watching idiots dance on TikTok. You can worry all day/month/year trying to determine what the best allocation is for your stock mutual fund portfolio or worry about which direction the market is going. Or you can just act and get the job done.

    Do not even bother with bonds until you are ten years out from retirement, or 15 years out at the most. Bonds will barely beat inflation and will not give you any chance at becoming a millionaire on an average income. They are only effective at preserving your capital after you have made your fortune, and they are not totally risk free unless you only buy US Federal government debt. Bonds should be zero percent of your portfolio when you are in yours 20s-40s and should be 50% or less of your portfolio by the time you enter retirement.

    While stocks are volatile in the short-term, they will allow a retiree to maintain their nest eggs throughout their retirement. Bonds will only guarantee you barely beat inflation, which is not enough to fund a sustainable retirement in most cases. Bonds are also not risk-free. US Federal Government bonds are safe, but corporations also issue bonds, and corporations CAN go out of business and default on their debts. Once you start transitioning a part of your portfolio into bonds, you should invest most of your "safe" investments into US Government and agency bonds.

Once you start investing, you are going to buy mutual fund shares like clockwork every month, using an auto-draft from your bank account. Once you start your auto-draft, you are going to let it run and not worry about how your portfolio is doing at any point in time. Regardless of whether we are in a recession or a huge economic expansion, you are going to just chug along, buying shares of your funds on a consistent basis. This is called dollar-cost averaging, and although it seems too good to be true, it is actually a very good strategy because it takes the guesswork and self-sabotage out of your investing strategy.

Many investors think they are brilliant and can predict short term fluctuations in the market, but that is demonstrably false; most of them completely fail at it. When you try to time the market, you tend to buy shares when times are good, and the market is going up and sell your shares when the market crashing. This is the exact OPPOSITE of what you should be doing; you ideally want to buy shares when they are on discount and sell them when they are at all-time highs. While that is ideal, it is impossible to predict when the market is at all-time highs.

Why is the market so hard to predict in the short-term? Because it is an emotional roller-coaster. From day to day, the market is highly reactive to the news cycle. A simple tweet from the President about <u>possible</u> tariffs can spook shareholders whose companies are heavily reliant on imports, leading to a fast crash in stock prices. Could this possible tariff hurt company profits in the short-term? Sure. Does that mean you sell your stocks based on the short-term news cycle? NOPE.

If you are a long-term, buy and hold investor who does not need to sell their stock for 30 years, a temporary tariff is meaningless. If you own a basket of great companies that have consistent earnings growth year over year and have long-term viability, those companies are going to be worth much, much more when you sell them in 30 years. A bad year or two because of a tariff is just a blip.

Do not follow the crowd. The crowd buys and sells at the worst possible time. If you buy consistently and HOLD your investments, you will buy in the good times AND in the bad times; over time, this evens out. It also takes the stress out of investing altogether. If you believe the world is going to be prosperous in 20 or 30 years, buy US stock mutual funds now and do not sweat the small stuff. Even if your diversified portfolio drops by 40% or 50% over a year or two, keep calm and understand the market ALWAYS comes back. If you crack and sell your stocks during bad times, you have failed. Do not do it.

At the end of every quarter, bi-annually or annually, you will need to rebalance your portfolio to keep it in line with your target asset allocation. For example, if you have a 33/33/33% small-mid-large cap mutual fund stock portfolio, the differing annual performance of each asset class will skew your portfolio more heavily toward one class. When you look at your portfolio at the end of the year, you might have a 35/30/35 asset allocation. You would then sell shares of the over-weighted portion of your portfolio and buy shares of the under-weighted portion to get back to the 33/33/33 breakdown.

This is a good thing, because large caps might do good one year, while small caps do better in another. By periodically rebalancing your portfolio, you are taking profits on out-performing sectors in one year and using that cash to buy shares on discount in another sector. Or you could just invest in a target retirement fund, which does all that for you.

How much should you invest? Most gurus say at least 15% of your pre-tax income, but I recommend as much as you possibly can. The more you invest, the faster you reach retirement. You can retire when you can sustainably live off your investments indefinitely without reducing principal. For an easy calculation, multiply your desired MONTHLY income in retirement by 300; this factors in a 4% annual withdrawal rate from your retirement assets. That will give you the amount you need in today's dollars to sustain yourself forever.

For example, I want $6,000 a month in retirement income. $6,000 x 300 is $1,800,000 I will need invested at retirement. While $1,800,000 may seem a lot, I will also have a pension and social security, which means I can still attain my desired retirement income without having to have $1,800,000 invested in mutual funds. If my pension and social security add up to $4,000 a month, I only need $600,000 invested at retirement ($2,000 x 300).

You will face similar math; to get to your desired retirement balance, you will need to invest in the right assets that will get you to your desired retirement balance at the right time. Every time you get a raise, instead of inflating your lifestyle, invest most of it. Sure, you can have a little bit of fun, but the more fun you have, the longer you will have to work before you achieve financial freedom. Try it out. If you get a $300 a month raise, save $250 of it and use the remaining $50 per month for fun. It will pay dividends in the long run.

I would love to hear you justify why you cannot start contributing to your retirement after you have read this chapter. I guarantee you are blowing you money right now on something stupid or meaningless that you can be redirected toward saving for your retirement. You may think retirement is far away, but it will be here before you know it. Investing is the difference between you being a broke, sad mess who is dependent solely on Social Security and Daddy Government and retiring with dignity. Imagine what it will be like to live on $1,500 a month with zero savings for the last twenty years of your life. Imagine the stress of trying to stretch that $1,500 to cover all your expenses.

After working hard your entire life, your reward is to spend the end of it broke and dependent. Do you want that? If you do not, INVEST. If you do, have fun being poor. Investing for your retirement has been made so easy now there is literally no excuse not to. If you do not want to think about anything at all, you can buy a low-cost Target

Retirement fund from Vanguard and set up an automatic investment every month. Do it, RIGHT NOW. Or be poor for the rest of your life, your choice.

Chapter 5: Do not Invest Like A Dude-Bro

Do not invest like a Dude-Bro. Dude-Bros are backwards-hat-wearing businessman wannabes. They tend to wear Oakley's with lanyards, pink visors, Vineyard Vines shorts and shirts and Sperry's. 93% of them are fraternity members who majored in either Business Management, Finance or Economics, graduating with a 2.89 GPA and get a job after college only because daddy is connected. These guys think they are hot shit, jumping from investing fad to investing fad with little rhyme or reason.

One day they will corner you and brag about their drop-shipping operation and their exploding revenue growth. The next, they will preach to you that Bitcoin is the currency of the future, and that you should dump every dime you make into it. Two days later, you will hear about the how shorting penny stocks can get you 200% annual returns. Basically, everything you hear coming out of someone's mouth that fits this description is a **toxic** threat to your financial success. They must be avoided and ignored at all costs. Do not be fooled by pointless bragging and flexing.

The successful investor invests in real estate, builds a profitable and sustainable business, or invests consistently in well diversified stock index mutual funds with broad exposure to global markets. That is how you get rich investing in America, unless grandma leaves you a surprise multi-million-dollar inheritance, which most people will not get. Dude-Bros are the human embodiment of the get-rich-quick schemes and easy money ideas that sound too good to be true, because they are too good to be true. Investing fads have always existed and will always exist, because they help a few people get very wealthy at the expense and ignorance of others.

Consider Bitcoin, a cryptocurrency or digital currency. Every Bitcoin transaction ever made is recorded on a transaction register called a blockchain. This blockchain is tracked and verified by every Bitcoin user, which makes it impossible for people to fake the coin or modify transactions; it most likely will never be hacked. Some people called bitcoin miners help verify these transactions and are rewarded for their efforts by receiving new Bitcoins. Bitcoins allow direct transactions between a buyer and seller across the world without using a real currency.

While Bitcoin is very intriguing, and cryptocurrencies can potentially grow to become a fixture of everyday life, the value of Bitcoin is solely based on supply, demand, and consumer sentiment. Bitcoin does not have any inherent value because it does not pay you; it is a commodity whose value is based solely on what people believe its value to be, not because of any inherent returns it produces. Your average Dude-Bro would have pushed you to "invest" in Bitcoin in 2017, the year that saw a massive spike in the value of Bitcoin. Between 2017 and January 2018, Bitcoin's value exploded from $1,000 to $19,783 as investor demand for Bitcoin hit a fever pitch. That is, until investors realized they were paying almost $20,000 for what was essentially a string of computer code. Bitcoin's value started crashing in January 2018, falling 73% in 2018.[23]

Fads like Bitcoin come and go. Sure, Bitcoin might be around and become a permanent fixture, but its value is based purely on speculation. It may also be replaced by another digital currency, or it may be shut down by governments around the world because they want control of the money supply. These are "investments" you want to avoid because you are gambling your money.

Compare a Bitcoin to a US Government Treasury bond. A Bitcoin is a digital currency. It does not produce an income. It just IS. Yes, it serves a purpose, which is to facilitate commerce through a digital medium, but it has no inherent value. There is no Bitcoin dividend. A Treasury

---

[23] https://www.barrons.com/articles/bitcoin-new-competition-is-on-the-way-51576621343

Bond is the exact opposite. Every 6 months, you will receive an interest payment from the Federal Government and at the maturity date of the bond, you will receive your initial investment back. A bond has a real, tangible, and predictable return. When you buy a Bitcoin, your only chance of making money is that sometime in the future another person will buy it from you at a higher price, simply because they believe it to be so.

Every time you hear someone promising you "guaranteed returns that beat the market" or "double your money in as little as 30 days," run away and do not look back. If everyone is talking about a new hot investment but cannot really explain what it does or how it makes money, it is probably a scam. The United States' Securities and Exchange Commission is constantly identifying new frauds designed to leach the meager savings of the dumb and gullible, but they cannot catch them all. 99% of the time, people have their entire life savings stolen because they believe they can get something for nothing and can get rich quick. That is not how life works.

As I have said repeatedly, you do not get rich quickly; you earn it through blood, sweat, tears and hard work. You either put in the work to build a real estate empire or business (the vast majority of which fail), or you consistently invest as much as you can every month into broadly diversified, low-cost stock index mutual funds.

Another great but predictable sin of the Dude-Bro is their ability to recommend the HOT STOCK TIPS, BRO. Individual stocks are a highly risky because they offer zero diversification. If you put your entire life savings in one stock, you risk losing everything if the company fails. What the Dude-Bro does is talk to his other Dude-Bro friends to get the latest "down-low" on supposedly up and coming companies that will grow immensely once the rest of the market magically learns its true value.

The company could be claiming any number of things, like developing the first fusion reactor that solves the world's energy problems, creating the world's first cure for cancer or creating tobacco free dip that rebuilds receding gum lines. These types of companies with big hype and unsubstantiated claims often draw Dude-Bro investors who think they are financial geniuses because they read about the company in a news article. These Dude-Bros will spread the word to their friends, who spread the word to their friends, slowly infecting hundreds, or thousands of people with hype. Investors begin to pour money into the company, and the stock skyrockets are more and more people are willing to pay ever more money for such a "great" company. Eventually, the company's claims turn out to be useless, the stock price crashes and people lose ungodly sums of money. These people get turned off from stock investing, firmly convinced it is a scam because they "lost it all" on a horribly diversified portfolio.

The lesson here is two-fold. First, do not buy just one or two stocks for your entire portfolio. Even the best companies and stocks can fall from grace and lose investors huge sums of money. Would you trust your retirement to just one or two companies? I would hope not. Sure, you might be rewarded if you are lucky enough to invest all your life savings into the next Apple or Microsoft, but that is highly unlikely. The risk of losing your life's savings broadly outweigh any rewards you might gain from getting lucky and picking a true winner.

Instead of buying one or two stocks, buy broadly diversified mutual funds that invest in hundreds or even thousands of stocks. Fidelity, a popular broker, allows you to invest a minimum of $0 into their mutual funds. With one dollar, you can invest and own a tiny piece of the entire world stock market, if you so choose. Compare that to one stock. Every company on earth would have to go out of business for you to lose your entire investment, which will not happen unless there is a nuclear war.

The second lesson is that you need to know what you are investing in. Dude-Bro might hype Bitcoin or a HOT STOCK, but if you do not know how it makes money, do not touch it. If you do decide to purchase individual stocks, keep it to no more than 5% of your entire portfolio and do serious research into the company you want to buy. You should read the company's Form 10-K, which is a required annual report by the SEC that contains the company's financial statements, management discussion and analysis and footnotes. This information will help you truly understand what the company does, how it makes money, how it spends its money and its plans for growth in the future.

You should also research the company's industry and competition to understand where your company fits in the industry. This research is the bare minimum you should do before you even consider buying an individual stock. Your average Dude-Bro will not know anything about new companies; they will just spread the hype they heard on YouTube or Reddit and contribute to unnecessary and unjustified hype for bad companies. DO YOUR RESEARCH.

What other "cool" and "sexy" fads should you avoid? Options trading, shorting stocks, futures contracts and more. Stock options are either "call options or "put options", which are contracts between buyers and sellers. You can use options to reduce the maximum loss you can sustain from a stock or ETF, or you can use them to speculate on the value of security. If you BUY a call option, you have the right, but not the obligation, to purchase a stock or ETF at a specific price, called the strike price. If you SELL a stock/ETF call option, you have the obligation to deliver a stock/ETF at the strike price if the buyer executes their call option. Call buyers pay a premium to the seller to compensate them for selling the call option for a fixed period. If you think a stock is going to rise over the strike price, you could consider a call option.

If you think the stock is going to stay below the strike price, you will sell a call option. Puts are the opposite. Someone who buys a put has the right, but not the obligation to sell a stock or ETF at strike price. The seller has the obligation to sell the security at the strike price if the put is exercises. Put buyers hope a stock/ETF falls in value, while sellers hope the stock/ETF will remain at its current value or increase.

Buying calls and puts can potentially reduce losses on investments. Selling calls and puts is a gamble to make money from premium payments from buyers; sellers hope they can collect premiums from buyers without ever having to execute call orders. There are tons of different strategies you can try to make money from options, but mistakes can cost you a fortune. If you do not know what you are doing, you can lose a little money on buying options, or a ton of money on selling options. Selling options is way riskier than buying because you are contractually obligated to fulfill a call or put, while buyers have a right, but not an obligation to execute their call or put.

If you are a long-term investor, there is no reason to dip your toes into the options world. Options are short term instruments to protect you from short-term loses. Why would you use short term hedging/speculative options if you are long-term investor with a time horizon over decades? YOU WOULDN'T. It is not worth making a quick buck here and there on options trading unless you have some play money you want to experiment with that is less than 1% of your portfolio. If you insist on listening to Dude-Bro and his stupid options strategy, which I do not recommend, only BUY options. Selling options can ruin you, because a wild swing in a stock's value could force you to buy a stock/ETF at a huge loss to deliver it to the buyer.

Now that you know to never buy or sell options, and you pledge to never do so because you are smart, the next Dude-Bro trading strategy you want to avoid is shorting stock. Traders short stocks they believe are going to fall in value. Here is an example. Bobby Brosef reads a Reddit post about a Weed stock called Tokes, Inc. that is about to tumble in value. Looking to make a quick buck so he can buy a new pair of Oakley's, he opens a margin account with a brokerage firm and borrows 100 Tokes, Inc. stocks from the brokerage. He immediately sells the stock at $10 per stock for a total of $1,000. As predicted, based on pure luck, Tokes Inc. subsequently tumbles to $8. Bobby Brosef then buys 100 shares of Tokes, Inc for $800 and returns the stocks back to the brokerage. Boom, Bobby just made $200 before taxes, and takes his wins to buy a fresh pair of Oaks.

If you do not understand how Bobby made money from that short example, do not worry about it. Just know that shorting stocks can theoretically expose you to unlimited losses. If you sell borrowed shares for $10 each, but then the stock price rises to $20, you will lose $10 per share when you buy them back to return them to the brokerage. Why do you have to rebuy the shares and not wait for them to fall?

First, they may never fall below your desired price point, which means you will never realize your gain. Second, when you borrow stocks from a brokerage to short them, you must pay interest and fees to the brokerage to compensate them for loaning you the stocks. The longer you hold the borrowed stock, the more it costs you. Shorting is inherently speculative. You are betting the stock or ETF you are watching is going to fall in value; sadly, stocks and the market at large are unpredictable and will often do the opposite of what you expect it to. Shorting is only for short term, speculation on the value of a stock or ETF; these short-term bets are based more on emotion and hype rather than fundamentals. Shorting is a gamble. If you are a long-term investor, which you should be, STAY AWAY. You are bound to lose.

Buying or selling futures contracts is another no-go zone for long term investors. Futures contracts are between a buyer and seller. The buyer agrees to buy a fixed amount of a commodity at specific price at a specific time in the future. The seller does the opposite and agrees to sell the commodity at the specific price at the specific time. A future is not an option. Options give buyers a right, but not an obligation, to buy and sell or sell an asset at specific strike price. An option buyer can choose to just pay the option premium but never execute the call option.

Futures contracts obligate BOTH the buyer and seller to execute their end of the bargain. Futures are pure speculation. A buyer is speculating the market value of the commodity will be higher than the price they must pay for the commodity on the settlement date. They can then resell the commodity at the market price, or they can do a cash settlement in their favor with the seller. Cash settlements allow buyers and sellers to settle the transaction without delivering the underlying commodity. Imagine having to literally deliver 1,000 barrels of oil to someone. Hilarious. Anyway, you need to avoid these speculative investments; they are based purely on speculation and can cost you ungodly sums of money if you guess wrong.

This leads us to the final "investment" in this Chapter you should avoid. Goooooooooold and other shiny rocks. Yes, it is shiny. Yes, it has been around for millennia. Yes, some financial experts recommend it (usually ones that have ownership interests in gold brokers). Ignore them. Gold is a shiny rock. That is it. Sure, gold has some industrial uses, conducts electricity well and is durable, meaning it is not entirely worthless. But it has very little intrinsic value and its price is based solely on supply/demand and fear.

Gold is also pretty and shiny, which activates special greed receptors in the average human. These investors believe gold is an investment and a hedge against because for millennia, it has been used as a medium of exchange. When national debts explode, currencies become devalued and inflation kicks in, people rush to gold because they believe it is an inflation hedge. While there is some historic correlation between gold prices and inflation, it is not always the case. Historically from 1970 to 2020, gold prices have shown a strong correlation with inflation in some decades and not in others for a variety of different reasons.[24] Just know that gold is not a surefire hedge against rampant inflation.

Besides its moderate correlation to inflation, another disadvantage of gold is it does not produce an income like a stock or bond; it is literally just a pretty rock. Since gold does not produce a cash flow, you cannot calculate use any kind of cash flow analysis to project its future value. That means gold's value can only be defined based on supply, demand and what people perceive its value to be. This makes gold's price inherently speculative, which is a terrible way to invest for your future.

Consider this. As of June 2020, the current total value of all gold on planet is around $8.9 trillion.[25] That's about 1/4th of the ENTIRE US stock market's capitalization as of December 31st, 2019. Now be honest. Would you rather own a big block of gold that you can plop in your

---

[24] https://inflationdata.com/articles/2018/04/27/inflation-affect-price-gold/#:~:text=Gold%20bugs%20often%20fear%20inflation,gold%20would%20be%20virtually%20flat.

[25] https://www.goldeneaglecoin.com/Guide/value-of-all-the-gold-in-the-world

backyard, or would you rather own 1/4th of every single actively traded US company listed on all US Stock markets? Exactly.

Investing fads will always exist. New investment products will hit the market and entice investors to buy them because they are cool and sexy. That does not mean you should buy them unless you understand exactly what they are and where they fit in your long-term investment portfolio. Investing isn't meant' to be sexy. You are literally just buying ownership into a broad swathe of the actively traded stocks in the United States by buying broadly diversified stock mutual funds.

As the US economy grows, corporate earnings increase and dividend payments are paid to you and re-invested over time, the stock you own through your mutual fund shares will increase in value. When you buy broadly diversified US stock mutual funds, you are buying an ownership stake in the majority, if not all actively traded companies in the entire country. That is all you must do. Shorting stocks, options, gold investing and other "alternatives" are not necessary to achieve wealth.

Chapter 6: Do Not Pay Taxes on Your Investments

Taxation will significantly reduce your lifetime earnings and investment gains. You don't need to be a tax expert, but you need to be aware of the tax deductions you can use to reduce your taxable income, and to reduce or eliminate the taxes you pay on your investment earnings. No, there is no way to legally avoid paying taxes on ALL your income. Once you make over a certain amount, Congress is going to take money from you instead of giving it to you. And, no, I am not going to recommend some offshore tax haven BS; this is a brief overview of the various tax benefits in the law that can protect your retirement savings from being fleeced by the government. Excellent tax benefits include contributing to your 401K, IRAs, and College 529 plans.

Imagine you buy a diversified stock index fund for a lump sum of $100,000 in a taxable brokerage. Every year, your mutual fund will probably pay you a dividend and distribute short- and long-term capital gains, which will be taxed between 0-20%, or as ordinary income, depending on several factors. Even if you re-invest your dividend and capital gain distribution, you will still have to pay hundreds or thousands of dollars EVERY YEAR in taxes. Let us say you sell the entire mutual fund in 30 years for $1 million. Guess what? You owe taxes on all $900,000 in growth. If you pay the maximum capital gains tax rate of 20% and an additional net investment income tax of 3.8%, you are looking at a $214,200 tax bill. Your $900,000 just became $685,800, all because you did not buy your mutual fund in a tax advantaged account. And this may be a low-ball estimate of the taxes you'll owe; the wealth gap is increasing every year in the United States, and you may see changes in the tax code over the next few years or decades that increase tax rates on capitals gains and dividends.

You can avoid all this by investing your dollars inside tax advantaged accounts such as Traditional or Roth IRAs and your 401K. Let us break each one down Barney Style. Traditional IRAs, or Individual Retirement Accounts, were passed into law in 1974 and became available to invest through in 1975. Roth IRAs came about in 1997.[26] These tax advantaged accounts were created as companies began to dump pensions; the government wanted to incentive workers to save for their own retirements instead of getting old and becoming a burden to the State. IRAs give tax advantages. The Traditional IRA allows you to contribute $6,000 (2020)

---

[26] https://personal-finance.extension.org/what-were-traditional-ira-and-roth-ira-contribution-limits-in-the-past/#:~:text=IRAs%20were%20established%20by%20legislation,income%20in%20a%20given%20year.

per year in pre-tax dollars in cash to your account, which you can open at any brokerage in the country. The IRA itself is not an investment. You buy investments INSIDE the IRA. For example, you can buy any stock, bond, mutual fund and more available inside your IRA or you can buy the exact same thing in a regular brokerage account. The only difference is how the investment is taxed inside the IRA versus outside of it.

Once you transfer money to your Traditional IRA, you can buy whatever investments you want inside it. Any money transferred to the account is not included in your taxable income for the year. For example, if you make $50,000 a year and contribute $6,000 ($7,000 if 50 or older) to your Traditional IRA, the government pretends you only made $44,000 that year for tax purposes. That saves you several thousands in income taxes every year on the front end. Once you purchase investments in the IRA, they will grow tax deferred if they stay in the account. Every dividend, every capital gain distribution, EVERYTHING is completely tax-free.

If you buy a mutual fund within the IRA for $100,000 and sell it within the IRA for $1,000,000, you pay ZERO tax. Compare that to the $214,200 you would have paid had you sold the exact same investment in a taxable brokerage account and you can see how powerful the IRA's tax advantages are.

There is a catch to this tax benefit. The government wants to dis-incentivize withdrawals from the Traditional IRA because the account is intended for retirement; if you withdrawal any money from the account before 59.5 years old, you will pay taxes on the withdrawal and a 10% penalty on top of that. And that is a good thing, because the last thing you want to do is withdrawal from your IRA unless it is a true emergency; a down-payment for a stupid sports car does not count. After 59.5, you can withdrawal the money without the 10% penalty, but all withdrawals will be taxed as ordinary income.

For example, if you make $40,000 at work and withdrawal $20,000 at age 60, all $60,000 will be taxed as if it were wage income. Think about it this way; with the Traditional, you get a tax break on the front-end and tax-deferred growth inside the IRA after you make the contribution, but you'll owe taxes on any withdrawals you make on the back-end. The Roth IRA is the opposite. With the Roth, you get taxed on the front end, your money grows tax-free inside the IRA and your withdrawals are completely tax-free.

Going off the last example, if you make $60,000 a year and you contribute $6,000 to your IRA, you are still going to get taxed on all $60,000 in that tax year. You cannot contribute to a Roth IRA if your income is over $139,000; it is designed for commoners like you and me.

The Roth IRA is superior to the Traditional IRA. The choice between the two comes down to whether you believe your tax bracket will be higher in retirement or right now. While you may believe your tax bracket is higher now since you'll probably be making less income in retirement, look at long term trends of US political beliefs. With wealth inequality growing, politicians from a certain political party will begin to not only demonize the very wealthy, but anybody that has a healthy million or two in their retirement accounts. These politicians will do their best to tax the "rich" and punish anybody who scrimped and saved for retirement throughout their working lives with higher taxes. Just watch.

The Roth IRA gives you a chance at avoiding these probable higher tax rates in the future, since whatever balance you have in your Roth IRA at 59.5 is 100% yours to keep. The Traditional IRA also forces you to start withdrawing money at age 72 because they government really, really wants to start collecting the tax money. This does not happen in a Roth since the money was already taxed on the front end. Do the Roth. The tax-advantages are amazing, and if you max it out every year and pick good investments inside it, you are very likely to have a long, happy retirement.

You can open a Roth IRA at any number brokerages, like Fidelity, Vanguard, Charles Schwab, TD Ameritrade and more. I personally recommend Fidelity or Vanguard for their diverse index mutual fund offerings and low fees, but any of the other large brokers are fine too if Fidelity/Vanguard are offensive too. Fidelity has no investment minimums for investing, while Vanguard is famous for low fees. Avoid opening an IRA at a bank; they probably will not have many options to invest in, and the expense ratios on their mutual funds will generally be higher.

You can open as many IRAs as you want, but the maximum you can contribute every year is $6,000. You cannot do $6,000 in your Roth and $6,000 in the Traditional IRA; the $6,000 is a total for both accounts. You have between Jan 1st of the tax year and April 15th of the next year to fund your IRA, which means you have 15.5 months every year to contribute the $6,000 to your IRA. If you are not doing your best to max your IRA, you are smoking crack. Your IRA is an amazing wealth building tool, much like your 401K, if your employee has.

401Ks are offered by employers. You can start your own 401K if you are self-employed, but if you work for a company or small business, the 401K they offer must do. 401K is a reference to a Section in the US Internal Code that is cited as the legal basis for corporations to institute these tax advantaged retirement accounts for their employees. Some investment dork did not make up "401K;" it refers to a law that authorizes employers to offer tax advantaged retirement plans to employees. 401Ks are completely unrelated to personal IRAs, which means you can max both your 401K and IRA every year; their maximum contributions are not cumulative. Anybody can open an IRA if they have earned income, while a person must work for an employer who offers a 401K to be able to contribute to it.

If your employer offers a 401K plan, you can contribute up $19,500 a year. The added benefit of the 401K is your employer can match your contributions, and they do not count against your $19,500 limit. While you can only contribute $19,500 per tax year, your employer can contribute an additional $36,500 in matching contributions for a total of $56,000 a year. Not that they will, but it is theoretically possible.

401Ks have the same tax benefits as the IRA, they come in both the Traditional and Roth variety and you cannot withdrawal from them without penalty and/or taxes unless you are 59.5. I personally recommend the Roth 401K because there is NO income phase-out limit for contributions. You can make a trillion dollars a year in income, and the government will still allow you to contribute to your Roth 401K. This is not the case with the Roth IRA, which has an income limit. When you turn 50, your contribution maximum increases to $26,000 per year. This is a POWERFUL wealth building tool because the tax benefits are unbeatable. Once your after-tax dollars are contributed to a Roth 401K, all growth is tax free if you keep it there and withdrawal it when you are supposed to. You can avoid hundreds of thousands and of dollars in capital gains taxes by contributing to your 401K over the course in your life. You can also rebalance your portfolio in your 401K tax free whenever you want; if your investment was outside your 401K, you would incur a taxable event every time you sold an investment to rebalance.

The downside of the 401K is you do not pick what mutual funds/investments are offered within the plan. Your company does. While the tax benefits of the 401K are great, your employer might contract with a horrible investment management company offering high fee, low performing mutual funds. That is a serious downside a lot of people face with their 401K. This is not a problem with an IRA, because you can open one anywhere you want.

The best tactic with your investable dollars is to first get the matching contribution from your employer 401K. If your employer matches 5% of your salary dollar-for-dollar in your 401K, contribute 5%. This will instantly double your investment in your plan, even if your plan is absolutely trash. Once you get the match, max out your Roth IRA. Once your IRA is maxed, go back, and contribute as much as you can to your 401K plan. If by some miracle you max out both your IRA and 401K, which is a major accomplishment, any investable dollars should be directed to taxable brokerage accounts unless you are contribution to College 529s or Health Savings Accounts.

There is a little secret out there that not many people know about with the 401K called the Rule of 55. If you quit, get fired or laid off from a job in the CALENDAR YEAR you turn 55, you can withdrawal from your current employer's 401K penalty free. This means you can retire at 55 and start withdrawing from your 401K penalty free, but you must work until your age 55 to do so. If you quit at age 54 but you do not turn 55 until the next calendar year, you are screwed and will have to wait until 59.5 to withdrawal the money penalty free. If you roll your 401K into an IRA, you'll also have to wait until 59.5, and you can only use the funds in your current employer's 401K if you retire/quit/get laid off at 55 or after.

This is another tool in your tool-belt if you have your sights set on retiring before 59.5. One final note is that unlike the Roth IRA, which does not mandate Required Minimum

Distributions, you will be forced to take distributions from your Roth 401K after age 72.

Now all these rules and taxes may seem complex, but they really are not. Both your IRA and 401K are just holding accounts with tax advantages for the investments bought inside the accounts. Your employer provides your 401K and gives you limited investing options, while you can choose any broker and have many more options for your IRA. Each has a maximum contribution ($6,000 IRA vs. $19,500 401K), and both can be withdrawal without penalty at 59.5 (or 55 for the 401K if specific requirements are met).

You should NEVER withdrawal or borrow from your 401K before you reach your retirement age; it is literally the worst thing you could do. That money is there for your retirement only; it is not for you to blow on a ridiculous vacation or, worse, a CAR. If you take anything away from this, if you do not have an IRA, open one. Right now. If you work for an employer, ask about their 401K options. Not investing through these tax advantaged accounts is setting yourself up for retirement failure.

Once you have maxed out your retirement contributions for the year, consider funding a College 529 savings plan for your children. 529s are highly flexible, tax-advantaged investments accounts to pay for your children's college. Like the 401K, the term "529" comes from a section of the US Internal Revenue Code that gives the accounts their tax-advantaged status. Since their creation, every state in the US now sponsors a 529 plan. The beauty of the 529 is you can invest in any state's plan, regardless of where you live, and you can use the money in the plan to pay for allowable expenses at any state in the US. You can live in Virginia, contribute to Pennsylvania's 529 plan because you like its investments better, and use the money to send your child to college in California.

Some states will give you tax benefits if you invest in the plan of the state you live in, but that does not mean you have to limit your choice to one plan. The money in the 529 can either be used to buy pre-paid tuition at today's rates, or it can be invested in whatever mutual fund or other investment portfolios the plan offers to be distributed as cash for education expenses.

Contributions to a 529 grow tax-deferred, and distributions to pay for allowable educational expenses are Federally tax-free. Like I explained previously, when you sell an asset at a significant gain, you are going to get a huge tax bill that will severely reduce your return. The 529 prevents this from happening, if you spend the money in the plan on allowable expenses. You can spend the 529 money on tuition, fees, books, supplies, equipment, room and board for K-12, trade school, undergrad, graduate school and more. You can even transfer the beneficiary of the plan to another child or family member if the current beneficiary does not go to college. You can open a 529 plan for anyone, including YOURSELF, and you can stay in control of the account without any mandatory transfer of ownership to the beneficiary. Basically, these plans are the gold-standard for anyone that wants to pay for a family member's college.

The maximum contribution you can make to a 529 varies between each state and can range from $235,000 to $529,000[27]. You can contribute $15,000 per year without incurring a gift tax reporting requirement. You can also contribute $75,000 at once without incurring any reporting requirements to IRS for gift tax purposes as long you do not make any additional contributions for 5-years. This $15,000/$75,000 applies to one person for one beneficiary, which means you can contribute $15,000 per year and your spouse can contribute an additional $15,000 per year with no gift tax reporting requirements, PER beneficiary.

This method allows you to put a lump sum of money upfront to maximize investment compounding returns instead

---

[27] https://www.savingforcollege.com/article/maximum-529-plan-contribution-limits-by-state

of dividing it into equal installments over 5-years. As you can see, you can put a TON of money into these accounts to pay for college, but you need to be careful. Any withdrawals that aren't for qualified educational expenses are non-qualified and will be taxed as ordinary income with a 10% additional penalty. This is a savage penalty designed to discourage investors from contributing more money than is necessary to pay for a beneficiary's educational expenses.

You need to do your own research on your state's individual 529 plan to find any state tax benefits. If your state does not offer any state tax benefits, shop around other state's plans to find the best deal. When you open an account, you need to consult the plan provider to figure out what investments you should purchase in the plan that are best suited for your risk tolerance and for the beneficiary's time horizon. Do not be lazy and pick the coolest sounding mutual; know what you are buying and why. Finally, you do not need to go overboard with these plans if you do not have the money available. Your child's education is important, but your financial future and retirement is more important.

You may think your child's college savings are the priority, but will you think the same thing when you're old, broke and having to move in with your child because you can't afford to live by yourself? At that point, you graduate to intergenerational vampire status, which can do more harm to your child's financial future in the long run than a small 529 payment. Retirement is the number one priority, STRAIGHT UP.

My final note on 529s is you need to consult an investment advisor before you start investing in these plans. This book is a general overview of what 529 plans can do for you, but it is not a definitive source. I rant about many other things here and I do not have time to cover every single detail of what a 529 plan is besides the basics. Hopefully, this motivates you to invest a bit of your money in one every month for you beneficiary's educational expenses, which is my intent. You need to save for you beneficiary's college as soon as possible and allow investments to keep the account balance ahead of inflation.

It is better to invest $50 a month for 18 years than to save nothing and suddenly be on the hook for $20,000 a year in tuition for your precious, perfect child. That is how you to stay broke or send your kid off to college with no savings. If you feel obligated to pay for your child's college, started saving NOW. If you do not, you will either send them off to college with nothing, or you will be tempted to raid your own personal retirement savings to do so, which is a God-awful idea.

A complete list of all tax advantaged accounts available would be exhaustive. Just know this: TAXES BAD, TAX ADVANTAGES GOOD. Taxes are a huge drag on investment returns, and future tax rates are unpredictable. Long-term capital gain and dividend tax rates are low right now, but who knows where they will be when you retire. I personally believe taxes will skyrocket in the future to pay for even more government programs that a large portion of the electorate is craving for, but you can believe whatever you want.

The last thing you want to happen is to live frugally your entire life, saving diligently and picking great long-term investments, only to have your savings siphoned away by a high-tax, re-distributive Federal government. Pile as much as you can into your Roth IRA and 401K, and any leftovers can go into 529s if you have beneficiaries, to a reasonable extent.

Chapter 7: Only Get Married to Have Children. If You Do Get Married, Get a Prenup

Marriage's main purpose is to provide a solid foundation to raise children and make them functional members of society. **_Radical_**, I know. But that is what I believe, and you will not convince me otherwise. Since the primary purpose of marriage is to produce and raise children, in my 100% correct and flawless opinion, if you do not plan on having children with someone, do not marry them. Marriage provides a solid foundation for raising children, but it also opens you up to financial ruin.

A divorce will instantly strip you of half of your net worth or more, and potentially subject you to years or a lifetime of alimony and child support payments. That does not even include thousands or tens of thousands of dollars in legal fees you will have to pay, depending on the severity of the divorce. Divorce will destroy even the best laid financial plan. You could fund your Roth IRA, max you 401K and be well on track for retirement, only to get cleaned out by one event. Sounds terrifying, doesn't it? What if you could buy some insurance to give you a fighting chance of not losing half of your life's work for just a thousand or two dollars? Would you do it? Then get a PRENUP.

Prenuptial agreements exist to protect your current and future assets from pillaging by a vengeful spouse. For the average American, they will only cost $1,000 - $2,000, but even if they cost more than that, they are worth their weight in gold. I hear people talk all the time about investing and being smart with their money but refusing to spend money on a prenup because it is "too much money." These same people will spend tens of thousands of dollars over their lifetimes for car insurance or life insurance, which you most likely will not use, but will not pay a few thousand dollars for divorce insurance. Remember, divorce happens almost FIFTY percent of time. If you do not have a prenuptial agreement in place before you get married, prepared for a long, bitter fight for your money if you get divorced.

Prenuptial agreements are important to lay out exactly which assets/liabilities go to who in the event of a divorce. You can put all sorts of provisions in a prenup to ensure a clean divorce that protects you from getting raked over the coals. Just be sure to consult with your lawyer about your individual state's laws regarding what is and is not allowed in a prenup. Provisions you should consider putting in your prenup, depending on your state, include the following:

- Alimony waiver – Your spouse should waive all rights to alimony

- Protection of retirement assets and pensions – All assets in your name go with you in the divorce, including investment growth after the marriage

- Protection of assets brought into the marriage – You get to keep what you brought into the marriage. You should have a balance sheet listing all your assets/liabilities in the prenuptial agreement

- Inheritances – Each spouse keeps all inheritance money received from their own families

- Debt – Each spouse is responsible for their own debts incurred in their own names.

- Real Estate/Cars – Specify how jointly owned physical property will be divided.

These are just a few things you should consider putting in your prenuptial agreement. Make sure you both you and your spouse have your own individual lawyers review the final prenuptial agreement. <u>I am not a lawyer,</u> and you should not use this book as a legal primer on how to write a prenup. I just want you to get one and consult a lawyer who knows what they are doing so you can protect yourself from disaster. This will ensure both of you are represented fairly and will help your prenuptial agreement hold up better in court. Do not listen to people who claim prenups do not work. That's BS. Prenups can and do protect you and serve as excellent evidence to a divorce court showing that both spouses entered the marriage fully understanding how the property would be divided if the marriage ended in the divorce. They protect assets you bring into the marriage and protect assets you acquire in your own name after the marriage. The last thing you want to happen is to diligently save money throughout your marriage while your spouse blows everything they have, only to have your spouse claim half of YOUR personal savings for a "fair" divorce.

A counterargument I hear against prenups besides "they don't work" is that prenups set up a marriage for failure because you are "planning to end the marriage before you even start it." That is manipulative BS that you need to ignore. If your partner is strongly opposed to a prenup, especially if you have way more money saved away than they do, you need to question their motives for marrying you in the first place. Never forget, personal beliefs about prenups are largely based on self-interest.

If you have a $2 million net worth, you may be alarmed that almost half of marriages end in divorce and insist on a prenup before marriage. That is perfectly logical, because you're loaded, and you don't want to risk an almost 50% chance of losing $1 million. But consider the alternative. What if you were flat broke, in massive debt and engaged to a multi-millionaire? Wouldn't a prenuptial agreement be a huge negative to you? Even if you love your fiancé and want to marry them for reasons other than your money, the temptation will be there to resist signing a prenuptial agreement. Without a prenup, you have a greater chance of extracting those resources from your partner in a worst-case scenario.

This all my sound very cynical, but it is better to be safe than sorry when it comes to marriage and finances. Even if your partner legitimately loves you when you get married, when a divorce comes along, money fights will turn even the most loving people into vicious animals. If you have a high net-worth before you get married, do not fall prey to emotional manipulation from your fiancé or their family to skip over a prenup. Understand that humans always look out for their own self-interest, and there is nothing wrong with you doing so as well.

You should get a prenuptial agreement no matter what your fiancé or anyone else says, even if you do not have any substantial assets at the beginning of the marriage. You may not have a high net worth at the beginning of the marriage, but if you are financially aware and care about saving and investing, you will build significant assets or time. You do not want to lose all that just because your marriage failed after a few years. Prenups protect current assets and **FUTURE** assets, which is critical to your financial future.

Chapter 8: Children Do Not Have to Cost $250,000

Children will destroy your ability to accumulate wealth if you let them. I am sure you have all heard the statistic that each child you raise will cost you a quarter of million dollars over your lifetime. You must feed them, clothe them, keep them healthy, educate them and spend time with them, all which cost money in one way or another. You will undoubtedly have less money to save for retirement and other investments when you have children; denying that would be idiotic. What I will deny is that children are inherently so expensive that they are guaranteed to sabotage any chance at saving for retirement.

The mistake people make is that once they have children, they feel obligated to get a huge car, a massive house, buy their children the most expensive brand name clothes, enroll them in 20,000 different sports, private school and more. The mindset that your love for your children is directly proportional to how much you spend on them is a deeply flawed concept that needs to die in your brain if you want any chance of accumulating wealth.

Everybody wants the best for their children; you love them, and you want them to go far in life. You hope they do better than you ever did, in their relationships, financially, emotionally, and spiritually. You want them to be happy, which is a great thing to want. Everybody can agree on that, but what people will disagree on is how to get their children to that desired end state. Some parents spoil their children rotten, subscribing to the belief that dollars spent equals love. Other parents are much stricter with their spending, choosing to make their children work for their possessions to help them understand the value of hard work instead of showering them with gifts.

Even more parents are just lazy and let their children do whatever they want as long as they do not bother them. Regardless of how a child is raised, there is no guarantee a child will grow up into a functioning adult, but parents do have significant influence in what happens in a child's development. I subscribe to the belief that not spoiling your children, teaching them the value of a dollar and hard work is a much better strategy to mold them into functioning adults than showering them with gifts. This belief naturally leads to a lower overall bill to raise your child and leads to better results.

Out of the roughly $250,000 to raise a child, the largest costs are housing (27%), food (18%), child-care and education (not college) (16%) and transportation (15%).[28] To

---

[28] https://www.usda.gov/media/blog/2017/01/13/cost-raising-child

not spend $250,000 per child, your goal should be to reduce each of these expenses as low as practicable without endangering your family. Housing is the biggest expense, by far. The mistake people make with housing and children is they buy more house than they need. At most, you need ONE bedroom per child and one bedroom for mom and dad. You do not need any more rooms for guests to come visit. Screw the guests, they can stay in a hotel.

The median price for a three-bedroom home in the US is $246,321, while adding one extra room will cost you $347,148.[29] That's a $481.37 per month difference, which could be used to fully fund an IRA. When planning for children, do not factor in guests or extra bedrooms in your calculations. Your children will not be scarred for life because Uncle Bob has to stay at Holiday Inn for a week during his visit instead of sleeping in the house. If you really want to cut costs and have two children of the same gender, you could even buy a 2-bedroom home and make them sleep in bunk beds. I am sure your children are going to die if they must share a room with a sibling; it's basically child abuse, right?

---

[29] https://priceonomics.com/how-much-will-that-extra-bedroom-cost-you/

Saving money on food is easy. Yes, kids eat a lot, but you offset that by eating a home as much as humanly possible. Eating out is a luxury that will cost you a fortune if you let it. Compare spending $80 on a dinner for four to $20 to cook a chicken, mashed potatoes, and asparagus at home. Saving $60 for a little bit of work to cook dinner at home will help you control your budget. If you cannot afford to eat out and fund your retirement accounts, you do not deserve to eat out. It is as simple as that. If your budget requires you to eat at home all the time, you should also shop at the lowest cost grocery store in your area and buy everything generic or store brand.

For example, if you shop at Walmart you should only buy Great Value branded items whenever possible. Great Value is Walmart's store brand for thousands of different food items and costs much less than brand name items. If you find yourself overwhelmed with managing children and shopping, you can avoid impulse purchases at the store by ordering food delivery services through an app. Most major food chains offer delivery right to your home for a low flat-fee and small tip for the delivery driver. While it may cost more on the surface to order home delivery, ordering via phone is more dispassionate and helps you avoid impulse purchases you would have made at the store. This could help you save more money overall.

Child-care costs are tricky to reduce, especially if you have a two-earner household. Before your child starts pre-school, you'll have to pay an average of $991 a month for infant day-care and $847 a month for toddler day-care. Once your child starts going to school, you'll need to find a way to get child-care between the time school ends and the time you get off work. While you do get tax credits to offset these costs, the full cost is not covered by the government. You need to seriously analyze how much you are spending on child-care, because it might make more sense for one spouse to be a stay-at-home parent.

The last thing you want to do is have one spouse making less than money than the cost of child-care. In that case, it makes more sense for one spouse to drop out of the workforce for a few years. Yes, I know the culture at large are obsessed with both parents working, but do not feel pressured to have both spouses work if it does not make sense. If you haven't noticed, the culture at large is completely misleading when it comes to accumulating wealth by pushing endless consumerism; why trust the culture when it demands that both spouses work, when it puts you in the hole? Your best bet overall is to shop around and negotiate the price for the day-care center that suits your needs or have one spouse stay home if it makes more sense.

Saving money on child transportation costs is a no brainer. You do not need to instantly sell your current vehicle and buy a huge, brand new SUV or van just because you gave birth to a child. Your current car, even if it is a sedan, is going to be just fine to meet your transportation needs for your child. You are not being a good parent by blowing $30,000 on a brand-new car for two more inches of space in the backseat. Drive your current car if you can, and when you must get a new car, buy one that is used. This is covered in more detail in the car chapter, but you must understand that dropping tens of thousands of dollars on a huge, roomy for your children with TVs on the back of every chair is a great way to be broke for at least 18 years.

Once your children get older, they will eventually get to the age where they can get their driver's license. Whatever you do, do not buy them a new car once they get their license. Do not be tempted to buy a new car for yourself so you can give your older car to your kid to drive; that is the same as buying them a new car. If you want to buy your kid a car, do not spend more than $2,000, or even better, make them get a job and buy their own beater car. If you kid drives a garbage used car, it will save you a fortune in car payments and in car insurance premiums.

Housing, child-care, food, and transportation costs are all necessities to raising children. You cannot avoid spending a certain amount of money on these items, but you do have a choice in reducing the costs of these items to a reasonable level. What you do have much more control over is how much you spend on your children for discretionary items like clothes, vacations, toys, games and more. Spending on items that are unnecessary for the survival for your children is a huge expense that many people cannot seem to control.

Many parents believe that if they do not buy children the best name brand clothes, the newest iPhone, go to Disney World every year or give them fifty presents every Christmas that they are depriving their children of a good childhood. This is complete BS. On the contrary, dumping ungodly sums of money into trinkets to keep your kids happy teaches them that they need to always buy the best clothes and the newest gadgets every year to be happy. This behavior brainwashes your children into the cult of consumerism that will most likely follow them for their entire lives; this behavior perpetuates the **BROKE LOSER** mentality that keeps people poor their entire lives.

Sure, your children might complain because you bought them a $150 Android instead of $1,000 iPhone. They might call you a terrible mother or father because you took them to Marshalls or Ross for clothes instead of Hollister or American Eagle. Your broke neighbors might give you nasty looks or gossip that you're "poor" when you tell them you only took your children to Disney World once in their childhood instead of taking them twice a year. Girls might not want to date your son in high school because you made him buy his own $1,500 used Toyota Corolla instead of a new truck with a lift kit. What a TRAVESTY. They are broke, you are rich.

    Your children are going to be just fine without blowing all your money on garbage. A cheaper Android isn't going to kill your kids; the last I checked, a low-end Droid can place phone calls and send text messages. Polo shirts at Ross or Goodwill get the job done just as well as Hollister and American Eagle. Disney World once or twice a year is unnecessary, when there are so many activities you can do with your children that help them learn about the world without costing a fortune, like going to parks, museums, camping, etc..

    Think about it. Are you really doing your children a favor in the long run by spending every dime you make on buying them name brand junk that you throw away in a year or two anyway? Nope. If you do something that dumb, you end up not saving enough for retirement. This starts a chain reaction that leads to you becoming a financial burden and intergenerational vampire to your children when they are in their prime earning years. Deferring retirement savings to buy unnecessary garbage will leave you completely broke in retirement and force your children to take care of you. If they still like you and want to help you by that point, that is.

Buying your children lower grade electronics may also encourage them to get a job so they can buy nice things for themselves. You can use that as an opportunity to teach them about hard work and the power of deferring gratification to save money for long-term goals. You can also inculcate in them that pure consumerism is not a pre-requisite for happiness. Of course, your kids can completely blow you off and not heed your advice, but you can at least try to teach them good personal finance habits.

Now let us talk briefly about college. All I hear is parents freaking out about paying for their children's college. They raise their kids for 16 or 17 years without saving a dime for college, only to realize tuition and room and board a real thing once the acceptance letters roll in. That is ridiculous and short-sighted. One, you should start saving for your children's college as soon as they are born in tax advantaged accounts like College 529 or Pre-Paid Tuition plans. Saving

$50 or $100 a month over 18 years is much better than scrambling to find $20,000 a year at the last minute to pay tuition. Second, your children should attend community college and work part-time if they do not get full-ride scholarships or you do not have enough money saved to pay for a full-fledged 4-year degree at a University. If they complain about it, boo hoo.

Keeping them out of student loan debt is the greatest gift you can give your kids, which starts with pushing them to an affordable community college. Third, you should encourage them to consider a tour in the military. For just a few years of "fun and seeing the world" they qualify for amazing college benefits, like the GI Bill. Finally, encourage them to get a marketable degree in the STEM field. Following your "passion" is a sure-fire way to be broke. You know a better option? Get a STEM degree, do your "passion" on the side after work, and if it takes off and leads you to success, THEN quit your STEM job.

Now, you may think I am a terrible person for encouraging you to send you child to the military. You may think joining the military is a death sentence, or you may be a delusional peace activist that thinks militaries are unnecessary, and their abolition would lead to world peace. Whatever your beliefs on the military, it is by far the best way to pay for your child's education. If you failed to save for your child's college expenses, you cannot blame anybody but yourself if the military is the best option for your child to pay for college. If you are 100% opposed to encouraging your child to join the military and you haven't put anything aside for their college education, you better send them to the cheapest, lowest end school you possibly can. Your child does not deserve to go to an insanely expensive college just because they are your child; either save for their college to send them to an expensive school, don't save and send them to a low-end school, or send them into the military and let them go wherever they want.

Children will cost you lots of money, but you have a great deal of control over how much they cost you. You do not have to buy them the newest gadgets. You do not have to spoil them constantly. You do not have buy a huge house or a huge car. Teaching them how to be functioning adults that understand what hard work all is about is the great gift you can give them. Giving them everything because they exist, and they are your progeny does not set them up for success and it does not set you up for success either. If you are planning on having children, you need to have a well-thought out plan to control long-term costs; don't' just let life happen to you.

Chapter 9: Use Credit Cards to Build Your Credit Score and Build Wealth

Credit cards are an important component of wealth building. First, you need to max out every credit card you have, and then pay the minimum payment on it each month. This will cost you a ton of money in interest payments, but you will build a great credit score over time. Once you have a great credit score, you can qualify to take out more debt in the future at lower interest rates, which is a great thing. Your ultimately goal is to take out as much debt as you can and make consistent minimum payments to build your credit score. This holy credit score, which is inherently good in and of itself, is an important thing to have for the sake of having it. The higher your credit score, the more successful you are.

That was a **joke**, of course. You DO want to use credit cards to build your credit score and to get rewards points, but ONLY if you can control your spending and use them properly. Proper use means only charging normal expenses on the card you would have spent in cash anyway, and then paying the card "Statement Balance" off in full every month. Paying off your card in full every month will build your credit score; do not believe the toxic myth that you have to run a balance and pay 25% interest on your purchases to build your credit. That is a big fat lie that needs to die. A good credit score will save you tens or hundreds of thousands of dollars over your lifetime, and rewards points allow you get a 1-5% discount on every purchase you make. If you spend $30,000 a year on expenses, 1-5% off means you are saving $300-$1,500 a year to invest for your future. Credit cards are not free money to blow on BS you do not need; they are a tool to help you build a good financial future. If you pay one cent of interest on credit card debt, my permission for you to use a credit card has been revoked until you can grow up and use them properly.

Credit scores range from 300-850, 300 being the absolute worst and 850 being the absolute best. Lenders will look at your credit score to evaluate the risk to their principal they lend you and determine the rate they will charge you to lend you money. The lower your credit score, the higher the interest rate the lender will charge you. This higher rate compensates the lender for the higher likelihood you will default on your loan. Obviously, you want the lowest possible interest rate you can get, which means you want to present the rosiest financial picture possible to your lender.

For example, a FICO credit score of 740 will generally give you the best rate possible when you are shopping for a mortgage, which is crucial to your long-term financial well-being. The difference between in a 3% and 4% interest rate on a 30-year mortgage with zero dollars down is $139.53 a month in mortgage payments and $50,230.14 in interest payments over the life of the loan. A good credit score makes the lender happy because you are more likely to pay back your loan, and it makes you happy because you save hundreds of thousands of dollars over a lifetime.

Credit scores are evaluated using a variety of factors, which can vary depending on which company is giving you a credit score. Equifax, Experian and TransUnion are the big three credit score providers, and will each give you a different score depending on how they weight each category, but they will be close to each other. On average, 35% of your score is based on your payment history, 30% is based on how much money you owe, 15% is credit history length, 10% is based on new credit and 10% is based on the types of credit used.

Payment history is based on how often you pay your debts on time; if you never miss a payment, you will be fine in this category. For the amount owed, the lower your total debt owed as a percentage of your available credit, the better off you will be. For example, if you have $40,000 in accessible credit and you only have $1,000 in debt on a car loan, you are going to have a higher credit score than someone who has $35,000 in debt out of the same credit amount. It makes sense, because the more debt you have, the more interest you are paying and the higher chance you have of defaulting.

Your credit history length is important because it shows lenders whether you have been consistent over time with paying your bills. The longer your credit history, the better your score will be, assuming you make all your payments on time. The new credit portion of your score looks at how much credit you have opened in a short-time period. If you suddenly start opening a ton of credit cards, it may be an indicator you are having financial difficulties and you need access to more credit that you might be able to pay back. Generally, when you apply for more credit, you do not want to apply for a ton of a credit from different sources all at once.

Finally, the type of credit you use will affect your credit score. If you have experience with multiple types of credit, such as credit cards, car debt and mortgage debt and you pay your debts on time, it will positively affect your credit score.[30]

---

[30] https://thelendersnetwork.com/how-credit-scores-are-calculated/

You need a good credit score for two things: buying a home and financing a car. That is it. Credit cards that you pay off in full every month will help you build a great credit score you can use to leverage "good debt." The average person cannot and should not buy a home in cash, which means they must take out a mortgage to buy a home. Even if you could buy a home in cash, it is a terrible idea in the low rate environment of 2020 to use your cash to buy a home versus other, higher earning investment vehicles (stocks). A good credit score of 740 or higher will allow you to get the best interest rate you can possibility get on your mortgage. This frees up thousands of dollars a year in mortgage payments to invest in diversified stock mutual funds and build real wealth.

A good credit score does not mean you can afford MORE house. If all you need is a three-bedroom home for your family, that is all you are going to get. Your credit score, which lowers your interest rate and mortgage payment, does NOT mean you should buy a four-bedroom home if you do not need it.

Once you buy your home, when you are financially ready and it makes sense, you will eventually need to buy a car. As I have harped on constantly, you should buy a slightly used economy car and drive it until it literally falls apart. Cars are a wealth sink, but they are a necessary evil that you will need to budget for every decade or so. As long as you avoid buying new cars and avoid car payments like the plague, you'll be fine in the long run. When you do need to buy a car because your current car is truly falling apart, you should finance your car purchase with a five-year loan. With a great credit score in 2020, you can finance a used car for 3-4% interest per year, which is much lower than the historical 10% average return of the stock market.

Instead of paying $10,000 in cash for a used car, it is better to instead invest the $10,000 in a good mutual fund and make the monthly car payments for the term of the loan. The better your credit score, the lower your car payment rate and the less you must pay every month. This strategy works as long as you actually invest your excess disposable income in the stock market; if you take a car loan but don't invest your money, you might as well pay off the car loan quickly.

Once you pay buy your home and take out a car loan, your credit score becomes meaningless. The whole purpose of a good credit score is to get access to the best interest rates for credit you NEED. A modest home that provides a secure environment to live in is a need. Your used car that gets you from point A to point B safely is a need. Remodeling your kitchen because you want marble instead of granite counters is NOT a reason to improve your credit score. Getting the best interest rate you can on a fully loaded F-150 is NOT a reason to improve your credit score. Get it? Your credit score is just a tool, not a badge of an honor to brag about with your friends. A **BROKE LOSER** is someone how brags about their credit score because they do not understand its true purpose.

A great credit score proves you know how to handle debt, but it does not necessarily mean you are rich. A bad or non-existent credit score indicates you either do not use credit at all, or you suck at paying your debts back. But it does not necessarily mean you are broke. If you never financed anything your entire life but have a few million dollars invested in a stock portfolio, you would have a non-existent credit score. Get it?

Credit cards use is the perfect way to start building your credit score when you are young, as well as saving tons of money in the long run with credit card rewards. If you have no credit score, you can still qualify for either a student credit card, a secured credit card or a store credit card. Student credit cards are specifically marketed to students with .EDU email addresses and offer low credit limits, usually $1,000 or less.[31] If you're in college, Google "Best Student Credit Cards" and look for cards with Cash back rewards and no annual card fee. Once you get one of these cards, you want to charge only a small amount of recurring expenses to them every month, like your phone bill and Spotify bill. You will then set up an auto-withdrawal from your bank account to your credit card every month to pay off the "statement balance" on the due date.

Paying off the statement balance will avoid all interest charges, and since you are not a **BROKE LOSER**, that is what you will do. If you choose to pay the minimum payment instead, prepare to get screwed with interest charges and line the banker's pockets. Over time, as you pay off your credit card in full every month, you will build your credit score for future home and car purchases.

If you are not a student, you can still build your credit with a secured credit card. A secured credit card will require you to make a refundable down payment, which determines your credit limit. For example, if you make a down payment of $500, you qualify for a credit card with a $500 limit. The $500 down payment "secures" your debt; if you do not pay your bill, the bank takes your down payment. As with the

---

[31] https://www.creditcards.com/student/#:~:text=For%20most%20student%20credit%20cards,%2C%20and%20sign%2Dup%20bonuses.

student credit card, you want to avoid annual fees and you want to pay off your statement balance in full every month. While it may not initially make sense to use cash to secure a credit card, think for the long term. You want a good credit score for when the time comes to buy your forever-home and whenever your car blows up and you need a new one.

Keep that in that back of your mind if you have no credit score and want to build one. If you never build a credit score, you are never going to qualify for credit, and you're going to have a hell of a time buying a home and a car unless you have huge stacks of cash. To build enough capital to buy a home and/or car in cash, you will not be using that money to invest in stocks, which hurts your net worth in the long run.

Finally, you can use store-specific credit cards to build your credit score, but only at stores you need to shop at to buy necessities. These are generally easier to qualify for because stores want you to buy their stuff and charge you interest too. Just be careful what store credit cards you use to initially build your credit. Qualifying for a store credit card at the Gap or American Eagle (if they even have store credit cards) is stupid; buying name brand, over-priced clothes for the sole purpose of building your credit scores is a big no-no. Look for card offerings for stores where you buy necessities of life, like Walmart or Amazon credit cards. Every time you buy mostly "Great Value" brand groceries to feed your family at Walmart, charge your expenses to your Walmart credit card to qualify for discounts and build your credit. Every time you buy a necessary item and have it shipped to you by Amazon, charge it to your Amazon card. At the end of the credit period, pay off your cards in full. Boom, it is that easy.

I will say it again. <u>The primary purpose for using credit cards is to build your credit score.</u> This allows you to qualify for low interest rates when you finance large purchases that are a necessity for life, like cars and homes. That is it. An <u>ancillary</u> benefit of credit card usage is you can get discounts on everything you purchase throughout your life with credit card cash rewards points. Most credit cards in 2020 will offer a cash reward feature, usually with a minimum of 1% cash rewards for all purchases. Some cards offer more, some offer less. Some cards will even give you 5% cash back rewards for certain categories of purchases, like grocery stores, gas stations and others.

I encourage you to use these cards whenever you can, but not to abuse them. The 1-5% discount is great when it does not entice you to buy things you do not need. Getting 5% off on groceries does not mean you should buy 5% more groceries; you buy exactly what you need and reap the rewards. At the end of the billing cycle, you use your cash rewards to reduce your outstanding balance, instead of cashing them in and going to buy a meaningless piece of junk. Over the span of your life, this will save you tens of thousands of dollars.

Credit cards and credit scores are a magical thing, when used properly. If you cannot use a credit card properly and you use your high credit score to go into debt for ridiculous unnecessary purchases, you are a lost cause. You will be broke your entire life. Your income will not be used to buy assets, but instead line the pockets of bankers. You will barely be able to afford a house you need to grow a family if you can afford one at all. Creditors will hound you and your family daily, insulting you and shaming you for your financial failures. Do not be that person.

Use your credit card responsibly to build your credit score by charging essential expenses to it and paying your statement balance in full every month. Use that credit score to qualify for great interest rates for your forever-home purchase and for a used car, whenever you truly need one. You can get one of these credit cards as a student, by using a secured credit card, or by opening one at a store you frequent for essential purposes. Do that, and you are well on the way to success. Max out your credit cards to buy BS you do not need and have fun being poor.

Chapter 10: Ditch the Home with the White Picket Fence

I pull into my driveway and hit the garage button. The familiar rumble of the garage gears lets my son know I am home, and he bursts out of the garage door to hug me. I jump down from my truck with a lift kit, give him a big hug and carry him into the house. He squeals in delight, his little legs kicking in glee. My wife is in the kitchen, cutting up vegetables from Whole Foods for dinner. I give her a hug and a kiss and she smiles at me lovingly. I am winning at life. I am a public accountant working for KPMG. I just got my CPA license and a $4,000 bonus. My career looks bright. I make $75,000 a year and just bought a six-bedroom house for $500,000.

My parents and wife are proud of all I have accomplished. My mortgage payment is $2,300 a month, not including property taxes and insurance. All things being said, I pay $3,500 a month just to live my house when you factor in utilities and maintenance. I do not have much money left for anything else. We cannot afford to go on vacation to Disneyland every year, so we put it on our credit card. I can make the minimum payments. Right now, contributing to my 401K is out of the question.

*But none of that matters. I am a CPA; I DESERVE this house. I am successful. The fact I can barely afford to do anything except pay my mortgage and live off credit cards is irrelevant. The partners would never consider me for promotion if I lived in a place I actually could afford, like a disgusting townhouse. Gotta act the part so you can get the part, right? Plus, real estate always goes up. It is a great **investment**, and you build equity with every payment you make. I checked Zillow and my house went up in value by $5,000 last year. Sure, I cannot access that equity without taking a loan and paying interest, but I still made money, right? Everyone says buying a home is better than renting. I am moving up in the world because of this house. At least I am not a loser renter, am I right?*

Read this out loud: My house is NOT an investment. My house is NOT an investment. My house is NOT an investment.

MY HOUSE IS NOT AN INVESTMENT.

The most idiotic belief Americans hold is that owning a home is an investment, and renting is just throwing your money in the trash. Banks and realtors love this false belief because they make big money off it. Sellers pay 5.5%-6% of the home's selling price to realtors in commission every time they sell a home; think about how much realtors can make off a million-dollar home? Banks get to issue loans, charge loan origination fees and other costs to buyers, and then quickly sell the loan to investors to get the mortgage off the books. The more homes people buy, the more realtors and banks profit, and the more people lose their opportunity to build wealth.

A home is not a symbol of success. A home is a money-sucking, wealth-destroying liability that can ruin a person's financial future if they do not make the right decisions in the buying process. Yes, everyone needs a place to live, and you can either rent or own. But owning a home is not an automatic ticket to success, and it is not an investment. The argument that mortgage payments build equity over time, while renting does not, is a weak when you consider the additional costs landlords have compared to renters. Homeownership has a ton of hidden costs that people need to understand and factor into their budget before they purchase; if they do not, they will end up house poor with no excess cash to invest anywhere else.

There is nothing inherently wrong with owning a home. Owning a home can have many benefits, and in the long run you will pay off your mortgage, which is a key steppingstone to affording retirement. If you want to buy a home, you have done your research, found a good deal and you are financially ready, go ahead and buy. But understand your home is going to be a money sink and will probably cost you more over time than the equity you have built in the home. Your home is a liability, not an asset.

How does this make any sense, you ask? How could a home possibly not be an investment? The TV told me homeownership is almost always better than renting. That is generally true, in the long run. But what the TV likes to imply is that your home is inherently a great investment. It is not. It is a place to live that sucks up huge amounts of money for little return. Whether you rent or own, your monthly payment is not being invested into a financial instrument that generally grows over time, like a stock or a bond. You are losing money on each payment. Every, single, one. That is what I like to call a LIABIILTY.

Let us dive right into why owning a home is a money sink and a terrible investment. We are going to use a certain individual's recent home purchase as an example of how homes are a money sink, a necessary expense, a liability, whatever you wish to call it. This certain individual is yours truly, Christopher Alan Bell, hero of personal finance.

Last month I purchased my first home with a VA loan for $254,000. My interest rate is 2.89%, I spent $0.00 on a down payment (VA loan), and I do not pay private mortgage insurance (PMI). Just FYI, buyers are generally required to pay for PMI is they do not put 20% down as a down payment. VA loans do not require this because the loan is guaranteed by the government. PMI is generally paid with the mortgage payment, costs between .5%-1% of the home's value a year and is designed to protect the lender in the event you default. The lender requires this protection because someone who puts little to nothing down as a down payment for a home is more likely to default than someone who can afford to save up and pay 20% of a home's value as a down payment.

Most people do not get VA loans. You must be a veteran to even be eligible for one. If you are not a veteran, you must put at least 20% down on your home to not pay PMI. That is the first cost of buying a home. If you do decide to put 20% down, the return on your down payment is your interest rate. For example, if I put 20% down on my $254,000 home, I would put $50,800 down, and only need a $203,200 mortgage to buy the property. If I had not put the $50,800 down, I would pay 2.89% interest every year that additional loan balance.

That is a **weak** return that barely beats inflation. Compare a 2.89% annual return to the S&P500 stock index, which historically returns an average of 10% a year, compounded. If I had instead invested that $50,800 into a dirt-cheap S&P500 index fund, I would have a balance $131,762.12 after ten years. Conversely, the down payment on the mortgage loan would only save me $14,681.20 in interest over ten years. $131,762.12 vs. $14,681.20…which would you rather have?

The money you could have made from other investments that you instead spend on your home is called your opportunity cost. With a 20% down payment on my home, I would lose over $100,000 in potential gains in the stock market by putting 20% down as a down payment for my home. Sure, my mortgage would be lower with a down payment, but it would only free up a couple hundred dollars a month to invest in other assets. A couple hundred dollars a month invested into the S&P500 will not grow as quickly as $50,800 contributed in a lump sum or dollar cost averaged over a year or two, since there are fewer dollars currently invested in the index with the first approach at any one time. The wonders of compounding returns increase exponentially the more you have invested at any one time.

Your down payment is only one expense of your fabulous home "investment." Next, we have closing costs, or the upfront costs you pay to purchase your home. In my case, I spent $4,331 on closing costs upfront. Closing costs to purchase a home include paying for my mandatory home appraisal, loan origination fees, credit report fee, flood certification fee, prepaid interest, prepaid insurance and many others. On top of that, I was lucky enough to have the seller grant me seller concessions, and they paid around $5,000 of my closing costs on my behalf. If I had not gotten that I would have paid almost $10,000 upfront, just on closing costs alone, for zero equity in the home. Great investment so far, right?

It gets even better. I had to move into my new home, which cost $450. I had to buy a weed whacker and cord to put my fresh new back yard. I had to buy tools to reassemble my stuff, carpets to protect my hardwood floors, cleaning supplies and many other things. On top of that, I must start budgeting 1% of my home's value a year for maintenance costs that I would normally not have to pay as a renter. That is an additional $2540.00 a year I am going to spend with little to no return.

Oh, and one more thing. I bought a newly constructed townhome, so I did not have to drop any money on updated old or outdated appliances. That is a good thing for me, but the average home purchaser will most likely have to spend thousands of additional dollars fixing any broken or outdated appliances or fixtures as soon as they move in.

And I am not even done yet. My mortgage payment is $1,055 a month. Part of each payment goes to reduce my outstanding mortgage balance, and the other part pays interest. So, in the first year of homeownership, roughly $600 of my monthly mortgage payment is going to interest, and $455 is going to reduce my principle balance. At the end of one year, I have built up approximately $5,460 in equity for the low, low price of $12,660. Isn't that an amazing deal? I am going to pay $12,660 for an "investment" that will be worth $5,460 after one year. Can I sign up for a second!? This does not even factor in property taxes and insurance, which cost me an additional $283 a month. So, my first year's payments will total $16,056 or that sweet, sweet investment value of $5,460.

Now, some detractors might say that these costs are meaningless, since your home supposedly will always increase in value, offsetting the costs of ownership. This is false. First, the growth in your home value is a paper gain. Let us say my home value increases from $254,000 to $256,000 next year. What benefit do I get from that? Does that $2,000 increase pay put money in my pocket? Nope. On paper, I made $2,000, but I do not see a dime more in my pocket. I might even see an increase in my real estate taxes because my taxes paid are based on the assessed value of my property. The only way I access that gain is by either taking a home equity loan, which I will have to pay interest against, or sell my home. If I sell my home, I must pay up to 10% of the home's value in closing costs such as realtor commissions, seller concessions, repairs, moving costs and others. That is only $25,600 in costs to access $2,000 of growth in the first year. Great deal, right? Sellers generally will not make a single cent of profit on their home until they have owned the home for at least five years, not including the costs that seller paid to maintain the home.

Even if I somehow do eke out a modest profit by selling my home for more than I bought it for, factoring in closing costs, what will I do with that profit? I will need a new place to live, so I will most likely buy a new home in the area. Since home prices will have increased since I originally bought any gains, I achieved from selling my first home will go to pay closing costs and the inflated price of my new home. In some rare cases, home values do increase at insane rates, allowing the owners to sell for outrageous profits. However, this usually only occurs in overpopulated, dense urban areas like Los Angeles or New York.

If you do not live in a dense urban area or get lucky enough to live in an area where a large company decides to build a plant, you most likely will not see huge increases in your home value. Even if you do live in a such an area, it is not guaranteed that home prices will continue to increase forever and ever. Plan for your home's value to increase on pace with inflation; so, in inflation adjusted dollars, not increase in value at all.

Let us review how much I spent the first year of owning a home to see how wonderful this "investment" is. And keep in mind, I had the advantage of buying a new home that I did not need to spend money on to fix up. And I did not have to do a down payment. And I got seller concessions And I got an extremely low interest rate. You may not get these with your home, increasing your first year's losses on your "investment":

Analysis of Investment Return on First Year of Home Ownership

Expenses

Closing Costs - $4,331

Moving Costs - $450

Maintenance Costs - $2,540

Interest Payments on Mortgage - $7,259

Taxes and Insurance - $3,396

HOA Fees - $738

Total Cash Paid out of Pocket: $18,714

"Gains":

Equity in the first year from mortgage payments: $5,401

Home Appreciation (Assuming 3% per year): $7,620

Total (Paper) Gains: $13,021

Total Money in My Pocket: $0

In my first year of homeownership, I will pay $18,714 in cash, and in return I will receive $13,021 in home equity that I can only access through an interest-bearing loan or by selling my house. Assuming my home appreciates in value at 3% a year, which is a generous assessment. This "investment," in the first year, gave me a return of NEGATIVE 30%. I lost 30% of the money I put into the home in my first year of living in it. Man…what a great return!

Despite all the hate I am throwing at the investment potential of a home, I still think owning a home is a good idea for most people, if they make the right choices when you buy. This analysis does not pertain to someone who purchases a home with the intention of converting it into a rental property. Rental properties can and do make money for smart real estate investors who know what they are doing.

People can also lose money on rental property too; buying a home does not automatically mean you can turn around and rent it for a profit. You must know what you are doing, and you must be willing to deal with the hassle of tenants. The home you live in is not a great way to accumulate wealth in the long run. A home is a necessary evil and an expense that you must pay to survive, but it should never be thought of as an investment or a great investment vehicle to build your wealth efficiently.

That being said, there are some excellent benefits to owning a home. First and foremost, when you own your home, you will eventually pay off your mortgage. If you rent your entire life, you will pay rent until the day you die. Your total rent will increase every year based on the whims of your landlord and inflation. With a fixed rate mortgage, your mortgage payment will never increase. My mortgage payment is $1,055 a month in 2020, and it will be $1,055 a month in 2040. When you factor in inflation, your mortgage payment becomes more affordable with every passing year. Your property taxes and insurance premiums will likely rise with inflation, but they are only a small portion of your overall payment.

In the long run, anybody with a fixed rate mortgage will spend less of their income every year on their mortgage payment. Just do not be an idiot and get an adjustable rate mortgage (that is a story for another book).

You also build equity in your home over time. Yes, equity builds slowly, and every mortgage payment you make is a net loss, but you do get a small benefit from each mortgage payment. If you run a mortgage amortization table, you will notice most of your payment at the beginning of the mortgage is paying interest, but over time each payment pays down more and more of your loan principal. What you will see is a slow growth in equity for the first half of your mortgage payment term, with steadily increasing equity growth the later in the mortgage term you are. After 15 or 30 years, you own the home free and clear.

Even though its value at the point will be theoretical, you still have an asset with no accompanying liability that you can sell on the market if you need to. You also eventually pay off your mortgage, freeing up more money to spend on retirement or other investments…it just takes 15 or 30 years to do so. You can also itemize your mortgage interest payments on your tax return if you do not use the standard deduction. With renting, every dime you pay in your rent payment can be thought of as interest that does nothing to build your net worth. You do not get to write off any portion of your rent payment on your taxes; in that sense, you are flushing money down the drain.

Here are some general concepts you should keep in mind that will keep you out of broke-loser status with your home:

1. <u>Plan to buy one home and stay in it for your entire life</u>.

Buy your forever home. Only **BROKER LOSERS** buy starter homes. Starter homes are an excellent way to blow tens of thousands of dollars for nothing. Remember that closing costs to <u>buy</u> a home can be as much as 5% of your home's value and closing costs to <u>sell</u> your home can be 10% of your home's value or more. The costs are only one consideration for buying a forever home. You should also plan for your future. If you plan to have children, are you buying in an area with low crime and a good school system? If you are not, you may want to reconsider where you are buying. If you do not, you may end up having to sell your first home at loss to move to a better area once kids come around.

You are not a loser because you are renting. Renting is a smart thing to do if do not have the savings or income to afford to buy a home. Buying a home, you cannot afford is by far worse than renting. If you hear someone bragging about owning a home, they are a moron. Bragging about being a homeowner is like bragging about burning thousands of dollars bills every year to start your grill. Oh, and I am sure the neighbors will not gossip about you when you get foreclosed on because, by God, you were a HOMEOWNER for three months before that instead of a scummy renter.

2. Buy just the right amount of home you need to survive in the future.

Planning to have two kids in the future? You only need a three-bedroom home. Maybe a two bedroom if they are both the same gender. Screw the guest bedroom; guests can stay at a hotel. The less expensive your home, the less money you are dumping every month into a low/negative returning "investment." You want as many dollars as possible directed to purchasing assets (stocks/bonds/rental properties), not liabilities (your home/mortgage). Do not let other people's expectations make you buy more home than you need.

If you buy a large home you can barely afford to impress your friend and family, you are an excellent candidate for **BROKER LOSER** status. I am sure your children will hate you when you are able to afford to fully pay for their college because you did not blow all your money on a huge mortgage payment. Your wife will probably hate you too when you're traveling the world in retirement, because you will have a much larger retirement nest egg because you had money to invest.

3. Know Your Property Tax Rate.

You need to know what your property taxes will be. You can find it on your city's website or with a quick Google Search. You may have the option to see what your property's assessed value was last year to estimate your taxes. Look at previous property tax increases to predict what kind of tax increases you may see in the future. Your fixed rate mortgage will never change but increasing property taxes can significantly increase your monthly payment over time.

4. Budget for Maintenance Costs:

Maintenance costs have the potential to be overwhelming when you purchase a home. Need to replace a roof? Could cost you up to $15,000.[32] HVAC system goes out? Pay up to $12,000.[33] You may not have to pay these costs for many years, but they will happen eventually. You need to save diligently to meet these expenses, generally around 1% of the value of your home every year. In the case of my home, I should save $2,540 a year. If you forget to

---

[32] https://www.angieslist.com/articles/how-much-does-roof-replacement-cost.htm
[33] https://homeguide.com/costs/hvac-cost

budget for this, you will find yourself dipping into your 401K or IRA to pay for huge, unexpected home maintenance expenses because you do not have cash savings set aside.

5. LOCATION, LOCATION, LOCATION:

Buy in an area you could see yourself living in forever. Look for low crime rates, good schools, a good commute to work, nearby stores and others. You are not going to find the perfect place that fits every one of your desired criteria, but also do not want to buy in a dangerous area, or in an area you cannot afford. Be smart and think long-term!

6. Get a Fixed Rate Mortgage at a Good Interest Rate:

You want a fixed rate mortgage. A fixed rate mortgage charges the same interest rate over the life of the loan. Your rate will never change, which means your payment will never fluctuate unless you refinance. If you buy with an adjustable-rate mortgage (ARMs), you will be in for a nasty surprise when your rate increases. ARMs offer a low, introductory teaser rate for a fixed period to lure you in, and then increase after a few years. The rate increase could dramatically increase your mortgage payment; you may start struggling and be unable to afford your home. This will never happen with a fixed rate mortgage. Cannot afford a home on a fixed rate mortgage right now? Getting a bad interest rate because of your credit score? Well too bad…you are going to have to wait until you can buy with a fixed rate, or do not buy at all.

7. <u>Use a 30-Year Loan</u>

Ol' Dave Ramsey is an outstanding personal finance guy, but he isn't right about recommending a 15-year mortgage over a 30-year mortgage. My current 30-year mortgage payment is $1055. If I had a 15-year mortgage, and assuming the 15-year rate would be 2.5% vs the 2.89% of the 30-year, the monthly 15-year payment would be $1,694. Yes, you are paying off your mortgage faster with a 15-year. But you are also only getting a return equal to the interest rate you are charged. In this case, 2.5% for a 15-year mortgage. Instead, with my 30-year mortgage, I have the freedom to invest the $639 extra in my Roth IRA and taxable brokerage investments. I can achieve historical returns of 10% of more with those investments, compared to 2.5% I achieve with a 15-year.

It is true you pay less interest with a 15-year vs a 30-year. But consider the effect of inflation on paying interest. I am paying 2.89% on my mortgage. Annual inflation in the USA hovers between 2-3% a year. If you calculate the present value of my mortgage payments over the life of my 30-year mortgage, I am effectively not paying interest at all. So why would I choose to save on "interest" payments when I am effectively not paying interest at all, and I can invest the difference in a much higher returning investment vehicle.

Finally, if I lost my job for a period, it would be much easier to make $1,055 mortgage payments than $1,694 a month. The 30-year gives me much more flexibility and allows me to survive longer while unemployed. You can also pay more than your minimum mortgage payment every month. If you feel like you want to pay off your home early, you can tack on more money to your mortgage payment every month on your 30-year mortgage, but reduce it back down to the minimum whenever you need to.

These are some basic rules you should follow when looking to buy a home. Resist the temptation to buy a large, expensive house. I know it goes against everything you have ever been taught, but the truth is the larger the home you buy on a fixed income, the more broke you are going to be. The larger the home, the more money you are tossing down the drain every month with maintenance costs, HOA fees, property taxes and more. A large home is a signal of financial insecurity. Instead of being jealous of Mr. or Mrs. "Success" with a huge home they can barely afford, you should shake your head and laugh at their stupidity. Buy a home that is just the right size for your current or future family you plan to have. If you buy too big or too small, you are going to be under pressure to sell at a loss, or you will be trapped in the home if home values are not increasing in your area. This requires a little bit of planning and foresight. I know you can do it.

Now let us pivot to my next favorite money sink, cars.

Chapter 11: Cars are Your Enemy

Women love my car. I drive through town, windows down, blaring Nickelback at max volume. My Oakley half-jackets gleam in the intense mid-summer sunlight. Heads turn when I drive by, drawn by the obnoxiously loud rumble of my exhaust pipe. Women flush and men feel envy when they see me on the road, wishing they could be a part of or afford what I have. There is nothing like a nice car to signal that you are a success, that you have made it in life. I sneer at broke losers who buy used Toyota Corollas or Ford Fiestas, because they obviously cannot afford to buy a nice car like mine.

How can you possibly impress teenage girls and financially illiterate teenage boys without having an awesome new sports car? Sure, I may be $60,000 in car debt for a car valued at $38,100 on Kelly Blue Book. Sure, I pay $850 a month on car payments, $250 a month for car insurance, and thousands of dollars a year on maintenance. Yes, I have nothing saved for retirement and $50 in my savings account. But who cares? It is only costing me 60% of my after-tax income to afford the car. That is the price of success, LOSER.

Sound like you? Well, congrats. You are a **BROKE LOSER**. Cars are the mortal enemy of wealth accumulation. Most Americans are broke, and it is due to car payments and associated expenses. All Americans must pay rent/mortgage, food, utilities and other bills out of necessity, but they do *NOT* have to pay car payments as a necessity. The average American spends $554 a month, or $6,648 annually on car payments alone. Add in $1,758 a year for car insurance premiums, $1,186 a year for maintenance, $1,500 for fuel, and the annual cost for one vehicle can exceed $10,000 per year.[34] Since the average American family has 1.88 cars[35] (we'll call it two for obvious reasons), some American families are potentially blowing around $20,000 a year on cars.

And where is all this money going to? To pay for an "asset" that will be worth around 40% of its original value after 5 years.[36] Imagine paying $100 for a stock and it drops down to $40 in five years. Great return, huh? In a technical, accounting definition, a car is an asset, but ol' Chris Bell can assure you; cars are a horrible liability in the realm of

---

[34] https://newsroom.aaa.com/tag/cost-to-own-a-vehicle/
[35] https://www.statista.com/statistics/551403/number-of-vehicles-per-household-in-the-united-states/
[36] https://www.carfax.com/blog/car-depreciation

personal finance. Avoid car payments like a fat lady avoids kale.

The idea that a car symbolizes your social status needs to die a horrible death. The car industry's advertising is so successful and pernicious, and Americans are so stupid, that they willingly destroy their financial futures by throwing a huge chunk of their lifetime earnings into pieces of junk, simply to signal they have status. **BROKE LOSER** status. In my ideal world, people would be mocked for buying new, expensive cars. There would be a part of the local newspaper dedicated to ridiculing local townspeople who bought a new car. Young women would swoon at the sight of a rusting Ford Fiesta or Toyota Corolla and snigger at shiny, new BMWs. Little boys would aspire to buy the cheapest, ugliest car possible to free up their future income to build true wealth.

That would be a logical world that glorified real wealth and success, but alas, most Americans are too financially illiterate to understand what it means to be wealthy. The average American has accepted they will have to lease or make car payments for the rest of their life. It is madness to pay off your car and not immediately buy a new one, right? You must get the latest and greatest model car every five years. People would make fun of you if you do not, so you better stay broke your whole life if you know what is good for you. This belief swindles the middle class American out of the opportunity to invest their way into the upper class and enriches stockholders of car companies (the rich). In a way, I benefit from this ridiculous belief, because I own shares of car companies through my mutual funds. Every time someone buys a brand-new car that immediately loses 20% of its value once it is driven off the lot, I reap the rewards through stock price appreciation and dividend distributions from my car stocks.

Are cars a necessity in the USA? In many cases, yes. People need to commute to work. Does a $50,000, fully loaded sports car qualify as a necessity? NO. Nobody has any business buying a $50,000 car unless they are already financially independent, have millions of dollars in the bank and have nothing else to spend their money on. The purpose of your car is to get you from Point A to Point B safely, nothing more. I am not telling you to go buy a $500 1970s beater car from your local redneck, but the thought of spending more than $10,000 on a car should make you sick to your stomach.

To do that, you will have to accept the fact you are going to have to buy a slightly used, dependable car that you are going to keep until it blows up, figuratively. Expect to have a car with 150,000 or 200,000 miles on it or more before you replace it. Sure, you can ignore my advice and keep buying brand new, expensive cars you can barely afford, but it is ultimately up to you whether you decide to accumulate wealth or stay poor your whole life.

What can you do instead of buying a new car? Buy a slightly used car with low mileage. Ideally, you want to look for a used car that is 1-2 years old, since car depreciation is front loaded in the first few years, and levels off over time. This is not an iron-clad rule, however. You can buy much older cars; the key factor you are looking for in your next car purchase is VALUE. Value is getting the best overall deal for your money, which you almost never get with a brand-new car. If you must spend an extra $2,000 upfront for a dependable used car that will save you $5,000 in repairs compared to other cars over the next few years, then do so. The price of a car is not only what you pay up front, but what you will pay in the future for maintenance, insurance, gas and more.

Kelly Blue Book (KBB) is the best place to research the fair market value of cars you are looking to purchase. KBB provides estimates of a car's market value based on its current condition and mileage. Understanding your car's KBB value will give you leverage in a negotiation with a dealer or a private party and is the best way to avoid getting ripped off. If someone wants more than the KBB value for your car, walk away. There will always be more cars for sale. KBB also publishes articles listing the best value for used cars each year based on their categories. For example, if you have children and need a van or SUV, you can scan through KBB's list and try to find similar cars in your area. If you need a small, dependable compact car under $5,000, KBB probably has a list you can browse for that, too.

What if you already have two car payments for two new cars you just *had* to buy to show off to your mommy and daddy? My only advice is to pay them off as quickly as you can or sell them and buy cheaper, used cars. While I do not recommend paying off your mortgage faster, you want to eliminate car payments quickly. Car payments, especially if you bought two new cars, will eat up a huge portion of your disposable income. If you can't sell the cars, your best bet is to tackle the car payment with the lowest balance with any extra disposable income you have, pay it off, and then add the money you were paying to the first car to the second car payment.

Once you pay off both cars, you are NOT buying a new car until one of your cars completely breaks down. I am talking about total engine failure that would cost you $10,000 to replace. You will not buy a new car because you may have to make two $1,000 repairs to your used car. A new car will cost you $20,000 or more. It is better to pay even a few thousand dollars a year in repairs for a used car than to buy a completely new one.

For loan durations, I recommend five-year car loans for used cars. If you focus on getting a used car that meets the specifications we just discussed, you will not pay more than $10,000 for your next car. The five-year loan gives you a lower payment and gives you more flexibility in exchange for a slightly higher interest. If you decide you want to pay off the car quickly, you can make extra payments on top of your minimum payment. If you have a rough month with other expenses, you can just pay the minimum car payment and make up for it the following month. Just make sure your lender does not charge a prepayment penalty for paying off your loan early.

Once you pay off your cars, consider dropping your comprehensive and collision coverage to significantly reduce your car insurance payment. Collision coverage will cover you for any damage you sustain from your vehicle from colliding with another vehicle or object, including rollovers[37].

---

[37] https://www.insurance.com/auto-insurance/coverage/comprehensive-and-collision-auto-insurance.html

For example, if you hit another car, get hit by another car, run into a telephone pole or flip your car, your collision protect will reimburse you any damages to your car in excess of your coverage. You want to read your car insurance policy to see what your deductible is and how much cash you would receive if your car is totaled. You can also call your provider and play around with different comprehensive and collision prices with different deductibles. In general, you are going to pay an average of $596 for collision, which will fluctuate based on your deductible and car. Comprehensive coverage protects you from events more outside of your control, such as a mudslide damaging your car or a robber smashing your window in. It will cost you an average of $192 a year.

If your car is worth only a few thousand dollars, and you have enough emergency savings to cover any major car repairs, you are self-insured and do not need to have comprehensive and collision coverage. You can drop it and save an average $788 a year, which you can use to either fatten your emergency savings to prepare for any possible car repairs, or to invest in assets for your future. Why spend almost $800 a year to insure a worthless hunk of metal? Insurance should only be bought to protect you from major financial catastrophes, such as your home burning down, totaling your brand-new car I told you not to buy, or dying early. Spending almost $800 a year to protect a paid-off car worth only a few thousand dollars is a complete waste of money. Your state will require you to maintain a certain level of liability protection, which is understandable, but comprehensive and collision are an easy expense to chop.

There's nothing more I can tell you about cars. Either you accept cars are a destroyer of financial success and stop buying them, or you keep doing what you have been doing and staying broke your whole life. The choice is yours.

Chapter 12: Fire Your Scummy Financial Advisor

Jeffery Weinerdick, CFP, financial advisor for Skeezy Investment Solutions, is flying high. Yesterday, he met his sales goal for the year, bringing in his twenty-fourth client to the Skeezy "family." Jeffery is just 25 years old and has only worked for Skeezy for two years. His first year on the job was a struggle, barely meeting his sales goals as he struggled to build his book of business in his new town. Now after two years of living off rice and beans, he has finally made it big. He has honed his craft over the last two years and knows just the right things to say to sell whole life insurance, variable annuities, loaded mutual funds and expensive asset management services managed by Skeezy's best and brightest analysts. His commissions this year will undoubtedly exceed $100,000.

But Jeffrey has a little secret. He personally invests in none of the products he sells to his clients. Deep down, he knows that whole life insurance is incredibly overpriced and that the average American does not need it. Most of the policies he sold were to clients who barely had enough income to afford them. But his commissions were great, so he bit his lip. He knows variable annuities come with incredibly high fees as a trade-off for their guarantees, allowing Skeezy to invest client's money and make huge profits. Jeffery memorized Skeezy's sales pitch for annuities and he knows how to use it, but he would not put his money in such an overpriced, illiquid product with huge fees. And loaded mutual funds? Why on earth would anybody want to pay 5.75% of their initial investment, upfront, to invest in an overpriced mutual fund? Jeffery invests in Vanguard and pays zero fees to invest his money, and the management fees he pays are one tenth the cost of what his clients are paying. Those juicy commissions though…

Jeffery suppresses his guilt. His clients need him, don't they? Sure, they are getting ripped off with overpriced, outdated investment products, but they wouldn't be investing at all without him, right? Surely, he couldn't charge a flat fee to design a financial plan for a client without being incentivized to purchase products that pay high commissions, right? That would NOT be profitable.

Salesmen cloaked as financial advisors are the scum of the earth. I am talking about the guys and gals in the neatly pressed business suits, twinkling eyes and slicked back hair who come to your house and invade your privacy to sell you garage products. They schmooze you, pretend to be your friend, and throw a company-approved, memorized sales pitch in your face to awe and seduce you to buy their garbage.

If you employee one of these thieves, ditch them immediately, with zero remorse and without hesitation. I mean literally, right now. Call your scummy advisor, tell them you will no longer be using their services going forward, and you want a plan by the end of the day to efficiently and effectively transfer your assets out of their management and into your own control. If you invest with First Command, Edward Jones, Primerica or your local Thaddeus McBumblebach, LLC commission-only financial advisor, run away now!

These advisors will screw you hard and will not even give you the courtesy of a goodbye kiss. They will put you in "amazing" products, including loaded mutual funds, overpriced annuities, whole life insurance, and overpriced asset management products. Most advisors are incentivized to sell you products that pay them the highest commissions, even if they are supposedly "fiduciaries." They are not to be trusted.

Commission only financial advisors are not the only financial advisors out on the market, but they are the majority. There are other advisory services out there whose advisors are compensated in a manner more conducive to you as the client. Financial advisors can be paid commission-only, a small salary plus commission, or fee-only. Commission-only advisors are paid via a commission when they sell a product. If they do not sell, they do not get paid. These are by far the most common type of financial advisor out there. Edward Jones is a good example. They love to knock on people's doors in hope of duping innocent people into blowing thousands of dollars on their fee-laden products.

The next batch of advisors receive a small salary and can earn additional commission on top of their salary. This salary will generally be small and may not be permanent, so they must also sell overpriced products to really make the big bucks. Finally, you have fee-only financial advisors, who will charge you either a flat fee or a percentage of your assets to develop a financial plan for you. Think services offered by big banks like Bank of America or JP Morgan, Fidelity, Vanguard and many others. Each batch of advisors has different incentives for products to sell to you that may or may not be in your best interests.

Consider the incentives of a commission-only advisor versus a fee-only advisor that charges a flat fee for their services based on the percentage of assets you own. The commission-only advisor will want to sell you products that pay them the highest commission, because they live solely off commissions. Even if a lower commission product might be better for your individual financial plan, the advisor will likely steer you into a more expense-laden, higher commission product. The advisor's parent company will also encourage the advisor to sell high commission products, because the company is compensated as well as the advisor whenever a product is sold. At the end of the day, the commission-only advisor will pursue you mercilessly, and load with you with overpriced products that pay them high commissions at your expense.

The products a commission-only advisor will push on you are loaded mutual funds, overpriced annuities, whole life insurance, and overpriced asset management products. Mutual fund loads are sales charges, pure and simple. For example, if you invest $1,000 in a mutual fund with a 5.50% front-end sales load, you will pay 5.5% of your investment, or $55.00, right off the bat to compensate your financial advisor for their "amazing," memorized sales pitch approved by their parent company. You can figure out which mutual funds charge these fees by scanning over their prospectus.

These mutual fund shares are generally called A Shares, so if you see an "A" or "Class A" in your mutual fund's title, it probably has a sales load. Your $1,000 investment instantly becomes a $945 investment right off the bat. To get back to a balance of $1,000, your investment will have to grow by 5.82% in one year. Investing with Class A shares instantly starts you at a loss, and they exist solely to pay your scummy financial advisor.

If you complain to your financial advisor about paying upfront sales charges, they will say "no problem" and recommend Class C shares instead. Class C shares do not charge upfront sales loads but screw you over time by charging higher annual marketing and distribution fees, known as 12b-1 fees. For example, if your advisor recommends you invest in an actively managed Large Cap Growth Fund, you can choose between Class A or C shares. The Class A shares will charge you (for example, they vary) 5.50% upfront, an annual management fee of 1%, and an annual 12b-1 fee (sales/marketing fee) of .25%. The Class C shares will charge no upfront sales load, a 1% annual management fee, and a much higher 12b-1 fee of 1%. With both, you either have the option of getting ripped-off on the front end, or over time.

And that is not all…a lot of mutual funds offered by advisors have back-end sales charges of 1% to lock you into investing in the mutual fund for years before they go away. You get hits with fees here, there and everywhere when you invest through a skeezy financial advisor. DON'T DO IT.

Just when you thought commission-only financial advisors could not get any worse, they screw you over harder by investing you in actively managed mutual funds. Actively managed funds are funds where the fund management team is trying to outperform a market index, called a benchmark. Index funds are designed to track a market index as closely as possible and will never outperform the index. For example, an actively managed Large Cap US Stock fund will most likely compete with the S&P 500 index with the objective of beating the S&P's returns. An S&P 500 index fund will merely buy the stocks in the index to match it perform.

While it sounds like it should be easy for a highly educated and experienced actively managed mutual fund management team to beat a simple, boring index, it rarely happens. Over the last 10 years, only 15% of actively managed Large-Cap US Stock mutual funds beat the S&P500 index, with only 8% beating the index over a 15 year time span.[38] That's just sad and a testament to how badly even the best investors in the world suck at beating the market over the long term. But of course, your financial advisor is going to put you into actively managed mutual funds, which have higher expense

---

[38] https://www.cnbc.com/2019/03/15/active-fund-managers-trail-the-sp-500-for-the-ninth-year-in-a-row-in-triumph-for-indexing.html

ratios and can't beat the market, because they can't justify their existence if they put you in index funds.

Why would you even use a commission-only financial advisor if they were just going to put you in boring index funds that had no chance of beating the returns of the market? It's just so, so sad how badly people get screwed by these advisors, when they could just go to a large organization like Fidelity or Vanguard, pay no sales commissions and a modest management fee to get professional, low-cost wealth management.

After hawking mutual funds with sales loads, your commission-only advisor's next goal is to sell you an annuity. It's a great deal for these skeezes to sell you annuities, because they can make up to 8% in commission on the amount you invest into it, which is a disgustingly high commission rate.[39] To keep it plain and simple, an annuity is income insurance. They insure you against the chance you burn through your retirement savings. If you purchase an annuity, you will get a check for life once it starts paying out to you.

You can either invest a lump sum into an annuity or pay into them over time. They either start paying you

---

[39] https://www.annuity.org/annuities/fees-and-commissions/

immediately, or they pay you after a certain waiting/accumulation period. They can either pay you a fixed amount every month for life, or a variable amount depending on the performance of a benchmark tied to it. When you die, the insurance company keeps whatever balance you have left over in the account. That is the down and dirty. Annuities are very complex and come in all shapes and sizes. I'm not going to give you a page 100-page presentation on annuities, I'm just here to tell you not to buy them.

You advisor will hammer you with a well-rehearsed presentation to convince you buy an annuity and line his or her pocket with a fat commission. It will even be a good presentation and will highlight the amazing benefits and guarantees inherent within an annuity product. Don't you want a guaranteed check for life? Don't you want guaranteed, tax-free growth every year? Don't you want to be exposed to a stock market index with all the upside and none of the downside? You just cannot lose!

Think about it, smart one. Doesn't this sound too good to be true? If your advisor is pitching a product that sounds like a miraculous answer to all your financial woes, there is going to be a catch somewhere. With annuities, the catch is insanely high fees and a cap on how much your money in the annuity can earn. Insurance companies know they can take your annuity payments, make way more money on them with their own investments, all the while charging you high annuity fees to offset the risk of you somehow getting the better of them. Then can then pay you benefits until you die, and then take the entire balance of your account for themselves. All because you are too scared to manage your own investments. You would rather have mommy and daddy insurance company manage your money for you and make a fortune on your cowardice and inability to manage your own money.

For example, let us assume you buy an equity indexed variable annuity with a $1,000,000 lump sum that starts paying you in five years. Equity indexed annuities are designed to give you returns that track a stock market index up to a certain limit and eliminate any chance of loss. In this example, this annuity stops you from taking any losses on your investment but caps your gains at 5%. Let us say over the next ten years, the index your annuity is tracking returns an average annual return of 10%. Sure, it may have some good years and bad years, but overall, it went up by an average of 10%.

What would your annuity's average annual return be? No more than 5% per year, because the insurance company will cap the amount of gains you can have within the product to compensate them for the risk, they are assuming in paying your annuity. A 5% return on $1,000,000 would net you $1,628,894.63, while a 10% return would net you $2,593,742.46.

See the difference in returns? You would give up almost a million dollars of investment growth because you are too scared to invest your own money and cannot stomach down years in the market. And guess who profits from your fear and cowardice? Your scummy advisor and the insurance company. Stay away from annuities. No matter what your advisor tells you, no matter how inviting they may sound, purchasing an annuity boils down to you giving up huge returns because you want mommy and daddy insurance company to manage your money for you. Do not buy them, EVER.

The fun does not stop there. After selling you loaded mutual funds and an annuity, the next pitch will be for you to buy a whole life policy. Your scummy, smelly financial advisor will do their best to guilt trip you into buying an insurance product you do not need. "Don't you want your family to be taken care of when you die? Don't you love your wife? She will be starving on the street if you do not buy this expensive policy, you know. Oh, and did I mention whole life has an investment component that grows tax free? Now buy this policy or you hate your kids." That is kind of how the sales pitch will go.

But what is whole life insurance? It is insurance that lasts your whole life. If you pay the premium on time every month until the day you die, the policy will pay out the face amount upon your death. In a standard whole life policy, the premium (your monthly payment for the policy) and death benefit (what your family gets if you die) are a set amount. The premium you pay goes to two things: the "cost of insurance" and a cash value account. The cost of insurance is based on your age and health evaluation and goes up every year; the older you are, the closer you are to death.

To defray that cost over time, the whole life policy takes a portion of the premium and invests it in a cash value account. This cash value grows tax-free over time, and later down the road you can take out a loan against it or cash it out if you wish. When you die, the insurance company pays out the death benefit only. Your family does not get whatever cash value was in the policy; that cash value was there simply to defray the cost to the insurance company and is included in the life insurance payout. For example, if you have a whole life policy with a $300,000 death benefit and $150,000 of cash value, upon your death your family only gets $300,000, not $450,000.

Whole life only makes sense for people that may have to pay estate taxes, also known as death taxes. You are only going to pay US Federal estate tax on any estate net assets in excess of $23,160,000. Do you think you will have a $23 million estate by the time you die? If the answer is no, then do not buy whole life insurance. Whole life insurance is garbage. It is 10x more expensive than term insurance, it does not build cash value for three years, the average cash value <u>guaranteed</u> growth rate is 1-2% and 80% of policyholders cancel their insurance within 30 years.[40] This product is a stinking pile of garbage. If you need insurance, get a term policy to cover you and your loved ones until your mortgage is paid off and your children graduate from college. A 30-year term policy is safe bet and is 10x cheaper than a whole life policy of an equivalent amount.

So why do commissioned financial advisors sell whole-life insurance? You guessed it, COMMISSIONS. Whole life pays outstanding commissions. Back in the day, I was a part of the problem; I worked as a commission-only financial advisor for a few months in my late twenties. I sold

---

[40] https://www.whitecoatinvestor.com/the-statistic-whole-life-salesmen-dont-want-you-to-know/

several whole life policies to poor, unsuspecting clients who would have been better off with term policies. If I sold a whole life policy with a $200 monthly premium, I would expect my lump sum commission payout to be roughly $2,000 upfront, and I would continue to be paid a portion of the client's premiums for years after. And I was not the only one that got paid; my boss got a commission for my sale worth about $600 just for being my boss, and my company got another commission from insurance company on top of that. Three different commissions worth well over $3,000 were paid for one policy that costs the client $200 a month. And the client paid for all it. What a deal for them!

You must resist financial advisors when they try to sell you whole life. They will pull out all stops to sell you a policy, because it makes them huge commissions. It is as simple as that. Their sales pitch will most likely be a pre-approved, memorized script provided by their company to maximize their chances of duping you into buying a policy. You should not be talking to one of these clowns in the first place, but if you somehow find yourself stuck in an office with one, endure the sales pitch and tell them NO.

If these advisors truly had your best interests at heart, they would sell you a low-cost, term life insurance policy that covers you through your target retirement date. They would then do their best to encourage you to invest the additional savings from not buying Whole Life into commission-free index mutual funds that fit your risk tolerance and investment time horizon. But of course, they do not do that, because whole life is just so awesome (for them). RESIST.

Finally, financial advisors will do their best to move you into their company's wealth management program. Commission-only financial advisors generally work for an investment advisor or brokerage that offer a special tier of investment services to clients with a certain level of assets invested with the company. This special tier of wealth management will be managed by a core investing team at the company's headquarters.

Instead of the advisor investing you in one or two mutual funds, your portfolio will be managed by a "hot-shot" team of fund managers at the company level. Multiple different portfolios will be offered to clients based on their desired risk tolerance and time horizon. It will be pitched as an exclusive investing option for an exclusive class of "high networth" clients such as yourself.

So, what's wrong with this? You may see a pattern here…it is the fees and commissions that come along with it. The advisor wants you to roll your assets into these investment portfolios because they receive a percentage of your assets every year in commissions. It can range between .25%-1% of total assets under management every year. That is not including underlying management fees for the investments you are buying into. Overall, you will end up paying 2% or more of your investment balance a year for investment returns that probably will not even beat the market. Or you could buy an index fund or two for 2000% lower fees and get better returns. But the advisor does not care about that. They just want to get a commission check every three months for literally doing nothing but selling you an overpriced, underperforming asset management program. Stay clear!

 Compare all these insane costs you pay going through a commission-only financial advisor to a fee-only advisor. One of these advisors might charge you a flat $2,000 fee to build you a comprehensive financial plan or charge you 0.3% of your assets under management every year to pick investments for you. The fee-only advisor is getting $2,000 regardless of what product they recommend to you. They have no incentive to sell you a product simply to bolster their commissions. They only want to make you as happy as possible, so you recommend their services to others, incentivizing them to recommend the most appropriate products for you.

The fee-only advisor that charges you a percentage of your assets under management every year wants your investments to grow as much as possible, because their compensation is based on the total value of your assets. The higher your investment balance, the happier you are, the more they get paid.

You can save a decent amount of money by avoiding fee-only financial advisors altogether. You can still use them, if you wish, but you need to understand the costs. Consider if you choose to invest with Vanguard's Personal Advisor Services®, which charges an annual fee of 0.30% on balances of $5 million or less in assets under management. This fee is on top of the expenses charged by the underlying mutual funds. So, if the Vanguard Personal Advisor puts you into a mutual fund charging 0.3% a year, you are paying a total of 0.6% a year in fees on your assets; 0.30% for the advisory fee and 0.30% (as an example, expense ratios vary) for the mutual fund.

If you have $500,000 invested with this service, you are paying $1,500 a year for Vanguard to manage your investments and $1,500 in underlying mutual fund fees. That is $3,000 a year in fees. If you just bought the mutual fund directly, you would only pay $1,500 a year, not $3,000. Over 10 years, that is $15,000 in savings in fees alone, not to mention the compound growth you lost on the additional fees you paid.

I know it can be scary to start investing. But that does not mean you have to get fleeced by commission-only salesmen to start building wealth. If you want to do more research on financial markets and investing before you start managing your own investments, I encourage you to use fee-only advisors like Fidelity, Vanguard, Merrill Lynch, Wealthfront, Betterment and others. Please stay away from the financial advisors that want to push whole life insurance, annuities and loaded mutual funds; they exist solely to rip you off.

If you decide to go with fee-only wealth management services, make sure you understand exactly how much you are paying in fees every year. These fees eat into your overall investment performance and can add up to hundreds of thousands of dollars over a lifetime of investing. Once you understand the investing world enough to strike out on your own, you can say goodbye to wealth management fees and start managing your own financial future.

Chapter 13: Student Loans are Toxic Trash

Timmy could not stand the anticipation. The garage door rumbled closed. Mommy was home! Timmy ran the stairs three at a time, almost knocking mom flat on her backside in the kitchen as she walked in the garage door.

"Mom, is it here? Is it here?"

Mom smiled and held out an envelope.

"Oh my god, oh my god," Timmy squealed, jumping up and down.

"Love you, Timmy. Open it," Mommy said!

Timmy did not hesitate, breaking the seal and pulling out the letter.

"Congratulations! The admissions board at The University of Phoenix is pleased to accept you..."

"I DIIIIIIIIIIIIIID IT," Timmy screamed, hopping up and down.

Mommy screamed even louder, and the two hugged, tears flowing all around. Timmy was going to college! Timmy was going to go far in life!

Timmy opens his eyes. Sunlight blares through the window slates, forcing him to roll over to prevent his retinas from frying. Another U of P dream? Of course. Timmy is not a dope, and would never attend an overpriced, garbage, scummy for-profit college like the University of Phoenix. He is doing it right. Living at home. Paying a small rent to his parents, doing chores around the house to earn his keep. He is attending the local community college for $125 a credit hour, which he pays for in cash. If he gets a 3.5 GPA or higher with his associates degree, he is automatically accepted to a nearby state school and will be eligible for multiple state grants and scholarships.

He will graduate with $0 in student loan debt in two and a half years. His friends all went away to expensive four universities. Sure, they are getting wasted and waving glowsticks at frat parties, getting STDs from hook-ups and are projecting to be $100s of thousands in student loan debt at graduation. They seemed to be having sooooooo much fun. They were LIVING LIFE...Timmy shook his head. He knew he was doing the right thing and would have the rest of his life to party. He needs to get dressed ASAP, or he'll be late to his accounting class.

You want to be like Timmy. Timmy is the next generation of intelligent Americans who will attend university without destroying their lives. Timmy has seen too many of his friends enslaved by years of student loan debt, living off rice and beans, crushed under the weight of high monthly student loan payments. He knows the path to a bountiful future means he must defer gratification in the form of skipping frat parties, on-campus housing and study-abroad semesters in exchange for low "status" on Facebook; he won't be seen as "cool" by his debt-slave peers. How sad.

His father, Ristopher Rell, taught him that only **BROKE LOSERS** go into unnecessary debt to attend college. He knows some people have rich parents that can afford to pay for their children's tuition, but he understands life is not fair and some have to work harder than others to succeed. Instead of whining like a Communist chump about privilege and the unfairness of society, he chooses the best option he can to avoid debt and get ahead in life.

The most toxic, unforgiving, soul crushing debt you can draw for yourself is student loan debt. Americans love student loans because they allow them to live a fake, debt-fueled party lifestyle at college. Lenders love them because they can charge sky-high interest rates on debt that cannot be discharged in bankruptcy. Parents are so ignorant about basic personal finance principles that they often encourage their children, their own flesh and blood, to enslave themselves to decades of high interest debt in exchange for a piece of paper. Students across the United States buy into the ridiculous myth that a college degree is a ticket to the upper middle class. While this is partially true, they forget to read the fine print which states, "As long as you finish your degree, land a job out of college and avoid student loan debt at all costs." Everyone knows that student loans are crushing America's youth; I am already beating a dead horse enough.

Your salary will suck right out of college. Even if you think you are going into a "great" career field that you are sure will make you a ton of money to pay off your debt, you are wrong. Whatever you think you are going to make out of college, cut it by 20%. The median college graduate thinks they will make $60,000 right out of college but ends up with a salary $48,800. Your expectations of a starting salary will be a disappointment, especially when you factor in average a monthly student loan payment of $393 eating into that salary.[41]

Assuming the new graduate is paying a roughly 20% effective tax rate, that student loan payment is consuming $491.25 a month of pre-tax dollars from the student's salary. You should expect that as the maximum you are going to

---

[41] https://www.forbes.com/sites/zackfriedman/2020/02/03/student-loan-debt-statistics/#378549d2281f

make out of college. Remember, you are most likely 22 years-old with zero experience in your career field; you do not deserve a large paycheck and you will not get one. Only delusional, entitled children expect the average compensation for their career-field right out of college.

Do everything in your power to avoid student loans. You can attend live at home instead of paying room and board, attend community college, work full-time while in school, attend a cheap, accredited online university full time or *GASP* you can join the military. Ignore the opinions of the millions of basic American **BROKE LOSERS** who will chastise you for skipping over a prestigious private University for a community college.

Prestige is not worth a lifetime of debt-slavery to a government body or private lender. Living on campus so you can bring Becky back to your room at 2am after a drunken frat party is not worth ten years of high interest payments. American Pie should NOT be driving force behind your decision to skip community college so you can experience the "real deal, bro" on-campus.

Living at home, if mommy and daddy let you, is crucial to avoiding student loans debt. The average student will pay $10,800 a year at a public school and $12,210 a year at a private school for room and board.[42] Over four years, that totals to $43,200 and $48,840, respectively. You can cut those numbers by 95% by living at home and attending your local community college instead. If you are fortunate enough to have a four-year university within driving distance, you save 100% of those board costs. Sure, you'll miss out on part of the "college experience," or your **BROKE LOSER** "friends" might laugh at you because they are strong, independent and living on their own, even though they are living on bank loans to survive. They might even have a hot girlfriend/boyfriend, and you may be a bit jealous because you are not living the Animal House college-life. But, oh how the tables will turn when you are out of college.

Once you graduate, you will have no debt and plenty of savings to move out of your parents' house. You will have your own apartment, or maybe even put a down payment on your forever-home. Meanwhile, your broke friends, who were so cool living on campus in college, will be living with mommy and daddy after they graduate because they cannot afford to pay their loans. You can then swoop in and steal their boyfriend/girlfriend; they would rather date someone who can afford their own place, anyway. You know, just to assert your dominance. Also, anyone that says college was

---

[42] https://www.valuepenguin.com/student-loans/average-cost-of-college

the best time of their life is generally a loser that accomplished nothing in their life. College can be a great time, but there is much more to life than drinking yourself to death every weekend.

If you do not have a community college or four-year institution near your home, you can still live with your parents and attend an online university. I do not even need to go into detail about this; attending an online university is a no-brainer and can save you tens of thousands of dollars. I recommend Western Governor's University (WGU) for 100% online schooling. WGU is a private, not-for-profit based in Salt Lake City, UT. The school is regionally accredited, which is the same credential your every-day rip off private university will have. Students can complete their classes at their own pace and earn "competency units" for completing their classes via proctored online exams.

Tuition is a flat fee paid every six months, and hovers around $3,500 for undergraduate degrees and $4,180 for graduate degrees. During each six-month semester, you can complete classes at your own pace; theoretically, you can complete your entire degree in 6-months. The school even gives out tons of scholarships every year for needy students!

$3,500 for an accredited undergrad degree? Pffft. That is not cool or fun. Just take out $100,000 in loans instead for "prestige" and "sick throw-downs."

You should have at least a part-time job when you attend college. If you are attending an online university, I argue you can do a full-time job. Remember, every hour worked during college translates saves several hours of work after college to pay off student loan debt. Students can work as Resident Assistants in college dorms in exchange for free room and board or work various work-study jobs on campus. Or you can work at McDonalds.

Whatever generates an income for you to defray living expenses or help you cover tuition. Yes, your life will be busy, and you will not have much time to party with your Dude-Bro friends. Yes, you will be stressed and miserable at times. But it is better to suffer for a short period now, than to suffer for decades after college because you did not put in the blood, sweat and tears while you are young.

You can also join the military right out of high school. Yes, you are going to get yelled at, and mommy and daddy might cry when the drill sergeants cart you off for several months of pounding. Yes, you might deploy to Afghanistan or some other crap hole. Your unemployed liberal sister might call you a fascist. Your pothead friends might call you crazy. None of it matters. The military is, hands down, the best way to earn a college degree and live like a king while doing it. We will address this topic in another part of the book, but in summary, the military will pay for your tuition up to a certain point while you are on active duty, and you'll get the Post 9/11 GI Bill benefit once you separate and meet time in service requirements.

Do not make excuses for not joining. Seriously consider the military, even if you do end of up hating it; it is only a few years of your young life, and it will set you up forever. The benefits are unreal when you get out. I know because I am a veteran.

Remember, the purpose of college is to teach you a skill that provides value to others in the real world. If you go the easy route and get a liberal arts degree, you are effectively worthless in the real world. People need other people who have unique skillsets to provide a valuable service to them in exchange for money; that is the foundation of society. Need your toilet fixed and you cannot figure it out yourself? Call a plumber. Need your kitchen renovated? Hire a contractor.

If college doesn't teach you a valuable skillset, don't attend college. If you do attend college and choose a skillset that truly helps you get a job, pick the cheapest accredited college you possibly can and avoid student loans like the plague. Even if it means delaying college for a year or two to save up money, do it. Screw everyone else and their opinions; most people are clueless debt-slaves. Do not be a **BROKE LOSER**; win the game of life by starting out strong, unencumbered by five or six figures of debt.

Chapter 14: Join the Military

Want to be set for life? Do one tour in the military, get out and reap the benefits. Or, if you like to deploy to a mind-numbing hellhole every two years, leave your family constantly, move every 3-5 years and get shot at, you can do your 20 years and retire in your late 30s or 40s with a nice pension for the rest of your life. On top of your pension for life, you will most likely get VA disability, which is a hidden money-making scam that a lot of people in the civilian world know nothing about.

The military can be a miserable experience if the culture does not fit your personality or interests, but it is something you can suffer through for a few years in exchange for a lifetime of rewards. If you have not noticed, I am a big fan of suffering and struggling a bit when you are young because it hardens you and better prepares you for overcoming obstacles later in life. The military is a great way to learn to suffer.

If you are young, join the military for one tour. If you are old, tell your children or grandchildren to join the military for a tour. You do not have to make it a career. Do a few years, qualify for all the benefits America loves to shower on veterans and get out. If you do end up liking it, you can stay in for 20-30 years and getting even more amazing benefits. Do not make any excuses for why you or children should not join. Yes, you will get yelled at either a little bit or a lot, depending on which branch of service you choose. But that is a good thing, because it will toughen you up and make any civilian job you get after the military seem like cake.

Yes, you will have to follow orders, but every job in the civilian world also requires obeying your boss. The military is more hierarchical and stricter than your average civilian company, but it is not an organization of robots. You will still be dealing with a diverse group of human beings from across the United States, each with their own personalities and interests. Yes, you will work long hours, but you will also get lots of time off. Every service member gets 30 days a year off for leave, and usually one four-day weekend a month. In the military, service members work hard and play hard.

There is a misconception that pay in the military is bad, which cannot be further from the truth. If you are enlisted and live in the barracks, your entire paycheck is going to be disposable income because your living expenses are covered free of charge by the military. Single enlisted servicemembers generally live in barracks on the base, and they do not pay rent or utility charges. Their health care is completely paid for and their food is provided by the military for free or deducted from a special, tax free food allowance. They have subsidized life insurance called SGLI that does not cost more than $25 a month for $400,000 of protection. Every necessity that most civilians must pay for out of pocket is completely provided for free by the military.

The mistake people your average, ignorant civilian makes is looking at a servicemember's salary and assuming that servicemembers must pay rent/utilities/food/healthcare costs out of it, which is completely wrong. You can theoretically pocket your entire base pay if you are cheap enough and still survive. And that is not just for lower enlisted soldiers. If you are a non-commissioned officer or an officer, your pay is much higher than a lower-enlisted soldier, and you can live off the base. The military covers your health care, pays you a tax-free food allowance and a tax-free housing allowance. These allowances effectively cover rent, utilities and a portion of your monthly food expenses, allowing you to pocket almost your entire base salary if you are cheap enough.

If you play your cards right, you have the potential to save tens of thousands of dollars on just a short stint in the military. Imagine not paying rent for rent/mortgage, utilities and health care out of your current paycheck. Think about how much money you could save and invest...that is the unique opportunity servicemembers have to build massive wealth and retire early.

Another common misconception is that the military is an ultra-strict organization where you march around all day, have no free time and are controlled by robotic drill sergeants and officer's sun-up to sundown. Think the basic training portion of *Full Metal Jacket*. This is a fiction. The only time you will be in a training situation even remotely like *Full Metal Jacket* is during your initial entry training, which only lasts a few months. You will get yelled at a little bit but have no fear; basic training for all branches of the military is much softer and gentler than it used to be. You will still be tired and stressed during training, but the training is designed for even the most out-of-shape civilian to pass. It is not that bad. You will also not be physically harmed in any way; hitting a basic trainee is strictly forbidden and will get the drill sergeant fired immediately.

Once you finish your initial training, you are assigned to your active-duty unit, which can be anywhere in the world. If you are enlisted, you will most likely get your own private barracks room on the base or split it with one other person. If you are an officer, you will have the option to either live off the installation, or in officer quarters on the base. Housing used to be horrible across the military, but it has gotten much better for everyone. Generally, the Army and Marines have the worst housing on-base housing while the Navy and Air Force have the best. But overall, all four branches will provide with average to great housing conditions on the base.

Once you get to your active-duty unit, if you are not attending a training exercise, you are mostly working a 9-5 job. Some jobs in the military require you to work 12-hour shifts or over-night when you are not on deployment, but most of the military works on a 9-5 schedule. Physical training intensity is based solely on what branch of the military you are in and the culture of the unit you are assigned to. For example, you might have an Airman in the Air Force that only does physical training one day a week with their unit from 7-8am, or you might have a paratrooper in the 82nd Airborne who runs 5 miles a day, 5 days a week from 6am-730am. If you do not want to work out hard, avoid the Army and Marines and go for the Navy or the Air Force.

Which branch should you choose? I recommend either the Army or the Air Force. The Navy is a terrible idea. See this quote from Navy.com "Specific underway schedules can vary widely. Normally ships will go to sea for **10 days to 2 weeks each month** for training operations in preparation for deployment. Extended operations away from home port can last up **to 6 to 9 months, and ships typically deploy once every 18-24 months.**"[43] You're going to spend the majority of your life at sea while you're in the Navy in cramped working conditions, working long hours, without ever truly getting down time. Even when you are not at war, you are still going to deploy on long sea-voyages every 1-2 years without ever seeing your family for months at a time. Compare that to the Army, where you might leave for a month or two ever year, but not 6-9 months at a stretch unless you are deploying.

The Marines are a bad choice, in my humble opinion, because they are always underfunded, have slow promotions for both enlisted and officers and are by the far the strictest branch of the military. You will also have to spend lots of time stuck on a Navy ship in cramped quarters. The Army offers everything the Marines does expect for the hoo-rah dragon slaying and brainwashing propaganda. If you want to be a ground pounding warrior, Army offers faster promotions, more military base locations and a slightly more relaxed culture.

When choosing between the Army and Air Force, the main factors are your temperament and desires. Want to close with and destroy the enemy? Join the Army. Want

---

[43] https://www.navy.com/what-to-expect/for-families

more of a support role for the exact same paycheck? Join the Air Force. The Air Force does have cool jobs, such as flying a fighter jet, but those are few and far between. Most likely, you will not be a pilot in the Air Force. Air Force careers include diverse jobs such as Nursing, Weather, Water and Fuel Systems Maintenance, Vehicle Maintenance, Security Forces, Signals Intelligence and many others. The Air Force places a heavy emphasis on studying for and passing technical exams that qualify you for promotions, while the Army considers many aspects of a Soldier's potential for promotion, such as physical fitness, marksmanship scores, leadership ability and general knowledge of military regulations.

If you are a more bookish person, the Air Force is a better choice. The Air Force is also known for its more relaxed culture, better living conditions and laxer physical fitness standards than the Army. I hate to admit this as an Army veteran, but I think I would have liked the Air Force much better.

The Army also offers a diverse array of jobs, called Military Occupational Specialties. You can be an infantry soldiers, tanker, artilleryman, human resources clerk, intelligence analyst, radio specialist, supply clerk and many others. You do not have to be a warrior fighting on the front lines, storming the beaches of Normandy or clearing houses in Fallujah, Iraq. In fact, most of the jobs in the military are non-combat related; most soldiers will never find themselves fighting in trenches or digging foxholes. That is the single most common misconception people have about the Army, and it needs to die. Regarding promotions in the Army as an enlisted man, being physical fit, always showing up at the right place at the right time in the right uniform and demonstrating maturity and leadership potential will help you go far.

Officers compete for promotions by getting better ratings on evaluation reports compared to their peers. Overall, the Army will be a better fit for someone than the Air Force if you enjoy a slightly more rugged and grimy lifestyle with worse living conditions on military installations. The Army also offers unique jobs that the Air Force does not have, such as infantry, armor and artillery. If you want to be a fighter, join the Army. If you want to be a support person, the Air Force is a better choice.

What super cool benefits does the military offer you that make spending several years of your youth potentially hating your life? After only one tour of service, you are eligible for the Post 9/11 GI Bill (Chapter 33), which completely pays for your college and room and board. You become more competitive for Federal government jobs through Veterans Preference. You get access to the VA Loan, allowing you to purchase a home with $0.00 down. You may get VA disability for something asinine, like ringing in your ears or stubbing your toe at basic training. VA disability is a monthly, tax-free pension for life that increases with inflation, and can range from a few hundred dollars a month to a few thousand.

You get military discounts for life at a multitude of stores, which adds up to massive amounts over the long run. The list goes on and on, but you can set yourself up for life after only a few years of fun in the desert sun.

The Post 9/11 GI Bill is the number one benefit offered to servicemembers. If the military did away with every other benefit, the Post 9/11 would still make it worth doing a tour in the military. You are eligible if you served on active duty during any period after September 10th, 2001. Additional requirement to qualify include:

- Served at least 90 days on active duty (either all at once or with breaks in service) on or after September 11, 2001, or

- Received a Purple Heart on or after September 11, 2001, and were honorably discharged after any amount of service, or

- Served for at least 30 continuous days (all at once, without a break in service) on or after September 11, 2001, and were honorably discharged with a service-connected disability, or

- Are a dependent child using benefits transferred by a qualifying Veteran or service member[44]

More GI Bill benefit is accrued the longer you serve. If you serve 90 days, you get 40% of your maximum potential benefits. You qualify for all 100% of benefits if you do three years total of service, which is less than the average tour of duty for one enlistment. If you get 100% of the GI Bill benefit, which most honorably discharged servicemembers will, your benefit will cover 36 months of academic training or the equivalent of four full years of college education. You can use it for a Bachelors, Masters, Doctorate and a multitude of other job training programs. It is an amazing benefit.

What exactly does the post 9/11 benefit cover?

---

[44] https://www.va.gov/education/about-gi-bill-benefits/post-9-11/

- **"Tuition and fees**. If you qualify for the maximum benefit, we will cover the full cost of public, in-state tuition and fees. We cap the rates for private and foreign schools and update those rates each year (Up to **$25,162.14** per academic year National Maximum. Most schools offer the Yellow Ribbon, which covers the difference).

- **Money for housing (if you are in school more than half time).** We will base your monthly housing allowance on the cost of living where your school is located. (Your monthly housing allowance could be thousands of dollars a month, depending on where you live).

- **Money for books and supplies.** You can receive up to $1,000 per school year.

- **Money to help you move from a rural area to go to school.** You may qualify for this one-time payment of $500 if you live in a county with 6 or fewer people per square mile and you're either moving at least 500 miles to go to school or have no other option but to fly by plane to get to your school.[45]"

You cannot beat GI Bill when it comes to paying for college. Not only do you get your entire tuition covered, but

---

[45] https://www.va.gov/education/about-gi-bill-benefits/post-9-11/

the Federal government will pay you up to thousands of dollars a month to cover your room and board, as well as $1,000 a year for books. You will live like a king, incurring zero dollars of student loan, while your fellow students are going into massive levels of debt, all because they came up with some BS excuse not to join the military for a few short years. Every servicemember who does their three years or more gets the same benefit. You can be a warrior with multiple deployments, or a paper pusher for your whole tour; you both get the same amount of money for college.

The military also offers free schooling at several service academies you have probably heard of, like the Air Force Academy, West Point and the Naval Academy. Instead of doing a tour in military to qualify for GI Bill benefits, you can go to one of these schools right out of high school. You will have four years of fun, military-themed college education, after which you get commissioned as a highly paid officer when you graduate. After graduation, you will owe five years on active duty, three years in the inactive ready reserve and then you are scot free.

If you don't want to live and breathe the military in college, you can do Reserve Officer Training Corps, which pays you a monthly stipend, book allowance, and covers your tuition at any regular college. For only a few hours of ROTC duty a week, you get your college paid for, and when you graduate you can choose to either do your time in the drilling reserves or active duty.

After you complete your initial obligation after commissioning via a service academy or ROTC, you will start accruing your GI Bill benefit. Imagine that! 8-years of college education paid for, just for serving a few years in the military.

Veterans Preference in the Federal government is another great benefit you get from the military. Federal government jobs are highly sought after because they have great pay, benefits, generous leave, a solid pension and 401K match, and generally cap out at 40 hours of work a week. You can browse USAJOBS.gov to see what I mean. Most jobs give you automatic promotions to GS12 or GS13, which pay very well for the number of hours worked. These jobs are difficult to get because the Federal government gives preference to veterans in the hiring process.

Job applicants are ranked on a point system. When a veteran applies, they are automatically moved to the top of the pack. If the veteran has any kind of VA disability, they are ranked higher even than regular veterans. This preference system makes it difficult for civilians with no military experience to compete with veterans for Federal jobs. It also means a veteran is a shoo-in for a Federal job if they are qualified and do not screw up the interview. If you want a job with great work life balance and a great pension, all you must do is serve a few years in any branch of the military, get a degree and apply. As a veteran, you will crush the competition, even if you just filed paperwork and never deployed during your service.

That brings us to VA disability, the biggest racket in American history. Before you get out of the military, your medical records are examined to see if you may have developed any service-connected disabilities during your service. If you claim any kind of disability, the military will send you to get evaluated to see if you qualify for a rating. Depending on the type and severity of your disability, which can be both physical and mental, you can be awarded a VA rating between 0-100%. Veterans who are 100% disabled can receive up to $3,684.00 a month, TAX-FREE, for LIFE depending on how many family members they have.

While you may think this is only fair for a veteran who was totally disabled during war, the truth is many disabled veterans have gamed the system to receive the highest rating possible. There is a whole network of scrooges, scoundrels, scumbags and shitheads who coach veterans on what exactly to say to get the highest VA rating possible.

Many veterans, who you may think are paragons of virtue because "THEY RAISED THEIR RIGHT HAND TO DEFEND MURICA," willingly participate in this scam. Claim you have PTSD, even though you never were shot at and never left the base? Boom, 30% disabled. Pretend you have erectile dysfunction? 20% for that. Pretend to have hearing loss? 10%. The list goes on and on, but it happens all the time. How do I know this? Just go browse any veteran forum on the internet. Go ask a veteran who seems perfectly healthy and functional what their VA disability rating is. It may shock you when a perfectly healthy veteran tells you they are "100%, totally disabled." Yea right.

Before you have a meltdown and attack me in a patriotic rage, YES, there are truly disabled veterans who suffer from horrible wounds, and I am not in any way mocking them in this book. Veterans that lost a limb, were shot, badly burned, or developed real PTSD deserve every cent of VA compensation they receive. But do not for a second think that every "disabled" veteran you meet is truly disabled. Every veteran knows a fellow veteran or ten who is receiving disability compensation solely because they learned how to game the system. Do I have hard numbers to prove this to you? No. But I am a veteran and I know so many people who really make me doubt the system is not a scam.

The reason I even bring up VA Disability at all is that, if you go to sick call or get injured in the military at all, you will most likely qualify for some level of VA disability. You must make sure your injury is documented, and I advise you keep a copy of your medical records for yourself whenever you go to the hospital or sick call. There is nothing wrong with claiming legitimate disabilities when you leave the military; if you qualify for any disability rating, you have secured a pension for life that increases with inflation. I highly recommend you get your medical records looked at before you separate. Just do not be a lying scumbag and pretend you have disabilities you do not have just to make more money. That is called FRAUD.

The final military benefit we will discuss is the VA home loan. You will be eligible for the VA loan if you do 90 days of active service, or six years of creditable service in the Reserves or National Guard. The beauty of the VA loan is you do not have to make a down payment on a home, and you will not pay Private Mortgage Insurance. Instead of dropping tens of thousands of dollars on a down-payment, you can invest that money in stocks and realize much greater wealth over your life. For example, if you invest $50,000 in a S&P 500 index fund and hold it for 30 years at a historical 10% return will yield you $872,470.11. If you didn't have a VA loan, you'd have to put $50,000 down for a $250,000 home purchase, which would tie up your $50,000 in illiquid home equity, and only reduce your monthly mortgage payment by $210.8. Even if you invested that $218.80 every month for the next 30 years, you would only have $416,498.87. Assuming you invest your savings, of course.

The one catch of the VA loan is the loan funding fee. Per the VA, the funding fee "is a one-time payment that the Veteran, service member, or survivor pays on a VA-backed or VA direct home loan. This fee helps to lower the cost of the loan for U.S. taxpayers since the VA home loan program doesn't require down payments or monthly mortgage insurance."[46] The VA funding fee is charged on the balance of the loan amount and does not include any down payment.

VA Loan Funding Fee:

	If your down payment is...	Your VA funding fee will be...
First use	Less than 5%	2.3%
	5% or more	1.65%
	10% or more	1.4%
After first use	Less than 5%	3.6%
	5% or more	1.65%
	10% or more	1.4%

---

[46] https://www.va.gov/housing-assistance/home-loans/funding-fee-and-closing-costs/

However, if you are a disabled veteran with any rating, you do not have to pay the funding fee. Which is another reason why you should get a VA medical examination when you get out, because it can save you thousands of dollars on your mortgage.

There are even more benefits available to veterans, but we have beat this horse enough. It is 100% worth it to join the military, even if you only do a few years of service. Remember, the vast majority of servicemembers are not front-line fighters; the majority of servicemembers are in support roles. Drop any stupid excuses or anti-war ideologies you are pulling out of your clown hat to justify not joining up. You may hate it, or you may love it. Regardless, it is only a few years of your life for a lifetime of goodies. If you are young, most of your peers will attend college, go into massive debt and struggle to find a job. If you join the military, you will get a solid paycheck right out of high school or college and delicious benefits to boot once you complete your service.

I can personally attest to the benefits of military service for what it is worth. I did not enjoy my service in the Army for various reasons, but looking back, a few short years of pain have set me up for life. It toughened me up, showed me what hard work really is and saved me $100,000s on my education. I made a net profit for getting my undergraduate and master's degrees instead of going into massive debt because my tuition and room and board were paid for, on top of a monthly stipend. I had a guaranteed job making over $60,000 a year right out of college. I got to jump out of airplanes and rappel out of helicopters. When I got out of the military, I got a small VA rating, a lifetime benefit that helps me pay the bills. I regularly get 5-10% off large purchases because I am a veteran. I just used my VA Loan to purchase a home with $0 down. All for a few years of BS. It is worth it!

Chapter 15: Exercise and Eat Healthy

What on earth does exercise and eating healthy have to do with good personal finance? EVERYTHING. To embrace the need to have good personal finances, you need to believe you will be alive and healthy enough to enjoy your future financial independence. What is the point of investing money in a Roth IRA or 401K if you do not think you are going to be alive at 59.5, or have any quality of life in your old age? Why try to build anything in your life if you believe your life is inherently meaningless? What is the point of dying a millionaire? I hear people question the need to develop good personal finance habits because they cannot imagine a future version of themselves.

They cannot imagine themselves being alive in their 60s or 70s, and that they will need to have income to sustain themselves when they are old and struggling to work. Most people just throw their hands up and say, "I won't live that long" or "I'm screwed." They live day to day, spending everything they make, because they have convinced themselves they have no future to live for. And if you do not exercise, eat like crap and live an unhealthy lifestyle, there is a kernel of truth to that belief.

Exercise and healthy eating will not guarantee you will be healthy in your old age, but they make it much more likely. That is a fact. People will make all sorts of excuses for why they do not exercise or give you an anecdote of somebody who worked out and ate healthy their entire life only to drop dead of a heart attack at 55. Sure, it does happen. But imagine two groups of 1000 people. One group works out consistently, eats healthy and gets plenty of rest every night.

The other group never exercises, smokes, drinks excessively, only eats fast food and are all morbidly obese. What group, on average, do you think will live longer and healthier? If you say the second group, just throw this book in the trash; you are a lost cause. If you rightfully acknowledge the first group that maintains good habits will on average live longer and healthier lives, you are a reasonable and logical person. You may keep reading.

Exercise and healthy eating will keep you fit and active until the day you die. Sure, your body will degrade naturally as you get older, but you can slow that process down by running, swimming, and lifting weights, or a combination of the three. If you maintain your wellness throughout your working life, you have got a great shot at being healthy and active when you hit your retirement date.

Once you retire in your late 50s and early 60s, you are at a point where you finally get to enjoy the fruits of frugality and enjoy your final few decades of life. You will be able to travel around the world, walk around foreign cities, visit your family and go on trips with them and anything else you want to do. If you are fit and healthy, this is a very real possibility. If you are morbidly obese with severe health problems, you will hit retirement and be unable to do anything you enjoy that involves physical activity. Exercise is the key to achieving a great retirement because it allows you to enjoy it.

Exercise is not just for your future self; it also improves your day-to-day life and gives you the motivation to pursue your goals. Exercise triggers endorphins, a chemical that reduces pain, helps reduce stress, reduce anxiety, improve self-esteem, increases muscle tone and strength, increases energy levels and improve sleep.[47] These positive feelings will improve your mood and clear your thinking, allowing you to better pursue your goals.

This directly translates into improved performance at work and better relationships with your friends and family, as you feel better about your life after exercising. If you feel better about going to work and have more energy while you are there, you are more likely to work harder and do a better

---

[47] https://www.webmd.com/depression/guide/exercise-depression#1

job. This translates to better performance and improves your chances at snagging that next promotion, which improves your financial position. Exercise truly is a miracle cure that helps beat down feelings of depression and hopelessness.

Exercise also makes you more attractive. I know, that is a radical thing to say in modern America, but it is true. If you cannot accept that attractive people are generally treated better than unattractive people, you are living in a fantasy land. What are the benefits of being attractive? TONS. Everyone knows that attractive people are treated better by everyone else. If you are a guy reading this, think about the pretty girl at your high school or college that you had a crush on. Were you very nice to her? Did you see her in a positive light? Did you feel compelled to do nice things for her? Was she "perfect in every way?"

Your behavior to her was directly affected by her physical attractiveness. This positive, fawning behavior carries over into the workforce and into your dating life once you leave school. If you are very attractive, you are more likely to get taken seriously at work, get promotions and people will treat you better, which in turn will positively affect how you view the world. If everyone is nice to you and smiles at you, wouldn't you believe that the world was a happy and positive place? Yep. Of course, not everyone is "attractive." If you are 5'2", 120 lbs., you are not going to grow into a 6'2", 220 lbs. mass of muscle because you start lifting weights and running. But you will become the best version of yourself, which is more than most people can do.

So, exercise and healthy eating makes you healthy, improves your mood, makes you a more attractive version of yourself, gives you a better shot at getting to retirement in good health, and can improve your longevity. It sounds too good to be true, which is why it is so hard to grasp why so many people refuse to do it. My belief is that most people are lazy and cannot get past the initial hurdle of getting on a consistent exercise routine. Exercise is "too hard." "I don't have time." "I only need to diet." I have heard all these excuses, and they are all BS.

If someone prioritizes something, they always find a way to make time for it. People will think it is not a waste of time to watch TV for two hours a night, but blanch and claim they do not have the time to work-out when confronted about it. Or they say exercise is for dumb meatheads who can't read books, when really, they are just justifying their laziness by claiming intellectual superiority. All excuses are BS. If you choose to exercise and stick to it, the rewards are amazing. Even 15-20 minutes of moderate exercise is better than nothing, and everyone can find time to do it.

So, what type of exercise should you do and how should you diet? I am by no means a work-out expert and dietician; this is a personal finance book. If you want to learn to work out, I recommend you join a local gym and hire a personal trainer and a dietician. The trainer can develop a workout plan for you, explain to you the major muscles groups and show you how to properly use the exercise machines. The trainer is your go-to person to learn as much as you can about exercise, and you better take notes, because you are paying for that knowledge.

Once you have learned everything you need to start your exercise journey, you need to start your workout plan and stick to it. That part is on you. The best way to stick to a plan is to just GO TO THE GYM. Once you walk in the gym and get dressed, you are most likely going to do your workout regardless of how you feel before you start. The battle is getting to the gym in the first place; once you walk in, you have won. Dieting is another realm entirely, but is just as important than exercise, if not more so. Do not do stupid fad diets or starve yourself; go see a dietician and learn how to really eat healthy.

Exercise and dieting are you entirely on you. If you want to give yourself a good shot at being healthy in retirement, you need to take dieting and exercise seriously.

You can blow this little piece of advice off, and there is a chance you might still be healthy well into your later years without following it. But any logical person knows that exercising and dieting increase the likelihood that you will be healthy and live a longer life. Nothing is guaranteed, but you can increase the chances you will be able to enjoy your retirement.

Do not listen to the idiots who mock exercise because they "know someone who never exercised and lived to 100." That does not disprove the fact that people who exercise tend to live longer. Do not make excuses, just do it. It will change your life forever if you develop a consistent workout routine, and it will set you on the path of enjoying a long, fruitful retirement.

Chapter 16: Have a Plan for Retirement

Retirement and financial independence are the end goal of accumulating wealth, but a retirement consisting of sitting on a beach every day for the last 20 years of your life isn't the end-all-be-all; the novelty will wear off quickly. You are theoretically ready to retire when you are financially independent; if you can stop working tomorrow, but still pay all your bills and generate enough income to support your desired lifestyle into perpetuity (forever), you have achieved financial independence. But that does not mean you have to stop working; if you love your job, there is nothing wrong with continuing to work to give yourself purpose, meaning and a sense of community and belonging to an organization. Achieving financial independence does not guarantee you happiness, but it will give you maximum flexibility to do whatever you have always wanted to do.

The mistake many people make is to fixate on achieving financial independence without considering what they are going to do once they achieve it. These people reach financial independence, quit their job, enjoy the first few months of freedom, but eventually get bored and choose to go back to work. If you start on the path to financial freedom, you need to sit down and sketch out a plan of what you would like to do once you achieve it. If you do not, you are setting yourself up for failure. Human beings are happiest when they are working toward achieving a goal and moving forward in their lives. If you stop moving forward in life or trying to accomplish new things, you stagnate and increase your risk of falling into boredom and depression. This is why you see 90-year-old billionaires like Warren Buffctt continuing to work and accumulate wealth; it gives him a sense of purpose to continue working. The wealth he has built is irrelevant; it is the process of working toward achieving the next goal and finding the next profitable business to invest in that keeps him going.

You want to be like Warren Buffett, able to retire and live off your investments but with something you do that keeps you occupied and working toward a goal. Financial independence gives you the opportunity to explore new creative avenues that you did not have time to do while you were working. Perhaps you want to try to write a fiction novel, or write a screen play, or take up professional photography. Maybe you've always wanted to hike the Appalachian Trail or run a marathon.

These are all examples of things you can do that will keep you working toward a goal and will keep you as happy as your genes will allow you to be. Choosing to sit around and do nothing will lead to stagnation, boredom and depression, which is the last thing you want.

You need to prepare for the social ramifications of leaving your job if you reach financial independence. While people like to imagine they would be perfectly happy never having to go to work again, they discount the social aspect of work and the meaning that work gives people. Working in an organization gives you a sense that you are an essential part of the team, and that you add value to your organization; this sense of belonging and utility gives you more purpose and meaning to your life than you realize.

Once you leave work, you will not be going in anymore, socializing with your co-workers, and working with other people to achieve a common goal. Even if your co-workers are not your after-work friends, they still contribute to your overall sense of belonging and socialization, since you interact with them eight hours or more a day. This all goes away if you decide to leave your job once you arrive at financial independence.

You may also find your friendships might fade away with some or all your friends who continue to work full-time. You'll find your old friends can't get away from work or home life to get out and spend time with you because they are still working and don't have the income to maintain the same financially independent lifestyle that you do. While you probably will not lose all your old friends, you may find that you lose something you used to have in common with many of them. Others might be envious of your financial success and fade away. This is a natural part of life; whenever you go through big life changes, you tend to move on and make new friendships with people who are in similar life circumstances. This is inevitable, and you need to be prepared for it. If you do quit your job, you need to find another social outlet so you can get out and interact with people you will have interests in common with.

To reiterate, the goal of financial independence is the freedom to choose what work you do and when you do it. It does not guarantee you will be perpetually happy, because leaving your job and retiring comes with a whole host of new problems you will need to be prepared to face. If you reach financial independence but you love your job, keep working! But if your job starts stressing you out, or you feel you have peaked on the promotion ladder, you have the freedom to quit at a moment's notice with zero financial ramifications.

If you are not financially independent, you are trapped in your current job because you need the earned income to survive. Most people are hesitant to leave their current job and take the risk of starting a new career because they are scared their new idea will not pan out; this worry is completely irrelevant if you are financially independent. If you want to quit your corporate job with great benefits so you can become a full-time travel blogger, you can do so if you are financially independent. If it works out, great! If it does not, you still have enough money saved to last your entire life without ever working again. I cannot think of a better position to be in than that!

Conclusion

If you follow the principles I lay out in this book, you will change your life forever. You can choose to scrape by financially your whole life, or you can make the conscious decision to follow my advice to get ahead financially and stay ahead. You can choose to be an adult and spend your money responsibly, or you can continue to live the life of an impulsive child and spend yourself into financial oblivion. You can listen to the peanut gallery that will always push you to live above your means, or you can ignore the brainwashed masses and build your fortune.

You can bow to corporate propaganda, which pushes you to mindlessly consume products to build "status," which makes more money for them, or you can see through the brainwashing the system pushes on you to keep you spending and poor. The choice is yours.

The benefits of getting your financial house in order are incalculable and will improve your chances of achieving long-term happiness in your life. Money cannot buy everything, but it can protect you from worrying about whether you next paycheck will arrive on time to keep you solvent. Money can send your children to college without forcing them to incur massive loads of crippling debt.

Money can give you the freedom to choose where you work and when you work; if you are financially independent, you will never have to stay at in a toxic work environment again. Money is an amazing tool; anyone that "lives their life" and ignores their finances is either living a fake, subsidized lifestyle on daddy's money, or has no idea that they never have money and live paycheck to paycheck because they've bought into consumerist propaganda hook, line and sinker.

The biggest lesson I want to convey in this book is that building something meaningful is not going to be easy; it will require blood, sweat, tears and patience. To make more money, you need to work more hours and/or study a new, more-highly compensated skillset in your free time. That leaves you less time in the short-term for leisure, but in the long-term you will earn more free time for yourself once you raise your income. If you are spending everything you make, you will need to make some adjustments to your lifestyle to free up income.

To build wealth over the long term, you will need to send a part of your paycheck every two weeks to an account where you will not be able to touch it for twenty or thirty years. You will need to have the mettle to survive bear stock markets without liquidating your portfolio and locking in losses. You will have to keep paying your term-life insurance premiums every month and never see the money again, all to protect your family from the unlikely event of your pre-mature death. It is very easy to get complacent and stray off the path of financial success; the true battle is ignoring naysayers and your own human nature to stay consistent over the long term.

    I wish you the best of luck in your future endeavors, and I hope my harsh and judgmental tone did not make you cry. I actually do care about you and want you to live a fruitful and financially secure life; I'm here to slap you into shape, not to coddle you and tell you it's okay to keep making stupid financial decisions. Thanks for taking time out of your life to read my book: I hope it serves you well.

www.ingramcontent.com/pod-product-compliance
Lightning Source LLC
Chambersburg PA
CBHW060828220526
45466CB00003B/1021